50

MATHS LESSONS FOR MORE ABLE LEARNERS

- Age-appropriate lessons to stretch confident learners
- Ideas to accelerate progress through objectives
- Bank of challenging brainteasers

AGES 7-9

Ian Gardner

Credits

Author
Ian Gardner

Editors
Sara Wiegand
Christine Vaughan

Assistant Editors
Margaret Eaton
Rachel Mackinnon

Illustrations
Jenny Tulip

Series Designer
Catherine Perera

Designer
Micky Pledge

Text © 2007 Ian Gardner
© 2007 Scholastic Ltd

Designed using Adobe InDesign

Published by Scholastic Ltd
Villiers House
Clarendon Avenue
Leamington Spa
Warwickshire CV32 5PR

www.scholastic.co.uk

Printed by Bell and Bain Ltd, Glasgow.

2 3 4 5 6 7 8 9   8 9 0 1 2 3 4 5 6

British Library Cataloguing-in-Publication Data
A catalogue record for this book is available from the British Library.

ISBN 0-439-94528-3
ISBN 978-0439-94528-8

The right of Ian Gardner to be identified as the author of this work has been asserted by him in accordance with the Copyright, Designs and Patents Act 1988.

Extracts from the Primary National Strategy's *Primary Framework for Mathematics* (2006) www.standards.dfes.gov.uk/primaryframework © Crown copyright. Reproduced under the terms of the Click Use Licence.

510
76
GAR

Contents

About the series

50 Maths Lessons for More Able Learners is a series of three books designed for teachers working with higher ability children within the daily mathematics lesson. Each title will address the principles of inclusion for more confident learners identified in *Excellence and Enjoyment: Learning and Teaching in the Primary Years* (DfES, 2004). Each book covers a two-year span of the primary age range: KS1 5-7 and KS2 7-9 and 9-11.

Each title consists of 20 short 'brainteaser' activities and 50 lesson plans, each with an accompanying photocopiable activity page. The activities cover many of the objectives in the Primary National Strategy's revised *Primary Framework for Mathematics* (2006). The lesson plans and accompanying photocopiable activities are designed to:
- set suitable learning challenges for more able learners
- accelerate progress through learning objectives
- provide tasks that are more open-ended or extended in time and complexity
- fit into the individual teacher's existing planning for mathematics.

How to use this book

This book begins with a detailed Objectives grid, giving an overview of the objectives addressed by each lesson. Teachers can also use this grid to track forward to identify appropriate objectives from later years where necessary.

Brainteaser activities

A bank of 20 brainteaser activities follows (with linked photocopiable sheets on pages 18-27). The purpose of these activities is to provide short, focused opportunities to stretch more able pupils. Where relevant, links to brainteaser activities are included on the lesson plans. However, they can also be used flexibly as required - for example, you may want to map similar brainteasers with the theme of a lesson, or extend learning as a homework or assessment task.

Lesson plans

To make the book easy to use, all 50 lesson plans follow the same format:

Learning objectives

Each lesson is written to address one or more of the PNS strands from Years 3 and 4. Where appropriate, objective links to Year 5 are also included.

Expected prior knowledge

This incorporates a brief summary of what children should be expected to know or do before starting each lesson.

Key vocabulary

Key mathematical vocabulary linked to the PNS Framework (2006) is presented for each lesson.

Activity introduction

Each lesson opens with a short introduction, designed to introduce the context of the lesson to the group (NB: these activities would not be suitable for the whole class). The introduction can also be used to review requirements in terms of mathematical understanding and to facilitate or scaffold thinking. Although the teacher will be at the centre of this section of the lesson, the main purpose is to pose questions and lines of enquiry for the children to develop during the main activity.

Activity development

Incorporating instructions for setting and developing the main activity, this section offers opportunities for children to explain their thinking, so a range of teacher questions has been included. It is intended that the teacher will be at the perimeter of the group, allowing the children to maintain ownership of the learning, but will be available for low-level interventions. These include making observations, highlighting teaching/learning points, providing hints or tips for solving problems, suggesting methods of recording and so on.

Review

This section is focused upon allowing children to explain their thinking or present their work, so that effective formative and summative assessment can be made. It also reviews all possible outcomes to an activity and summarises key learning points.

Next steps

At the end of each lesson plan, ideas are included for how to develop an activity further. These ideas include at least one modification to an activity designed to challenge children and extend learning. This section also includes links to thinking skills and ICT.

Characteristics of able children

An able child may demonstrate potential in a variety of ways:
- cognitive skills (for example, learning new ideas with extraordinary speed)
- speech and language, such as ability to follow a complex set of instructions
- learning styles (for example, logical approaches to problems)
- social, such as high expectations of self/others.

In mathematics, this might manifest itself through content (such as making links within and across different topics) and/or through process (for example, an aptitude for solving logical problems).

Interventions

In extending able learners through challenge, pace and expectation, it is also important to consider the value of breadth of content. Most of the activities featured in this book include themes that all children in the class are likely to be exploring, albeit at a lower level of complexity. This feature enables the able child or group to integrate with the on-going topics of the class, and this serves an important social function.

An able child represents a challenge in terms of establishing the nature and extent of support. Broadly speaking, an able child needs every bit as much focus on learning as any other child. Through intervention and discussion, an able child can begin to appreciate what outcomes are expected or valued.

Curriculum initiatives

One of the key objectives within *Excellence and Enjoyment* (DfES, 2004) was to support schools in taking ownership of the curriculum. This includes developing teaching programmes which support all groups, and in shaping the curriculum in ways which will maximise opportunity and achievement. Within this, the Primary National Strategy is seen as a vehicle to develop assessment for learning, providing knowledge about individual children to inform the way they are taught and learn. This book supports these aspirations by providing a measured approach to extending the more able child and, as appropriate, to engage directly with that individual in this process.

Title of lesson	Year 3 objectives	Year 4 objectives	Tracking forward Year 5 objectives
1. Nearest ten	**Use/apply strand:** Follow a line of enquiry by deciding what information is important. **Counting strand:** Round two-digit or three-digit numbers to the nearest 10.		
2. 100% effort		**Use/apply strand:** Solve one-step and two-step problems involving numbers, money or measures, including time; choose and carry out appropriate calculations.	**Counting strand:** Understand percentage as the number of parts in every 100 and express tenths and hundredths as percentages.
3. Code breaker	**Counting strand:** Order whole numbers to at least 1000. **Counting strand:** Round two-digit or three-digit numbers to the nearest 10 or 100.	**Use/apply strand:** Collect, organise and interpret selected information to find answers.	
4. All in proportion		**Use/apply strand:** Suggest a line of enquiry and the strategy needed to follow it; collect, organise and interpret selected information to find answers.	**Counting strand:** Use sequences to scale numbers up or down; solve problems involving proportions of quantities (for example, decrease quantities in a recipe designed to feed six people).
5. Teacher's orders		**Use/apply strand:** Solve one-step and two-step problems involving numbers, money or measures; choose and carry out appropriate calculations. **Counting strand:** Use decimal notation for tenths and hundredths; relate the notation to money and measurement.	
6. Big car, little car		**Use/apply strand:** Suggest a line of enquiry and the strategy needed to follow it; collect, organise and interpret selected information to find answers. **Knowledge strand:** Derive and recall multiplication facts up to 10 × 10.	
7. Target numbers	**Knowledge strand:** Derive and recall multiplication facts for the 2, 3, 4, 5, 6 and 10 times-tables and the corresponding division facts. **Knowledge strand:** Use knowledge of number operations and corresponding inverses to check calculations.	**Use/apply strand:** Identify and use patterns, relationships and properties of numbers or shapes; investigate a statement involving numbers and test it with examples.	
8. Multiple puzzle		**Use/apply strand:** Identify and use patterns, relationships and properties of numbers or shapes; investigate a statement involving numbers and test it with examples. **Knowledge strand:** Derive and recall multiplication facts up to 10 × 10, the corresponding division facts and multiples of numbers to 10 up to the tenth multiple.	
9. Multiple dominoes	**Knowledge strand:** Derive and recall multiplication facts for the 2, 3, 4, 5, 6 and 10 times-tables and the corresponding division facts.	**Use/apply strand:** Represent a problem using number sentences, statements or diagrams; use these to solve the problem; present and interpret the solution in the context of the problem.	
10. Three of a kind	**Knowledge strand:** Derive and recall multiplication facts for the 3 times-table and the corresponding division facts.	**Use/apply strand:** Identify and use patterns, relationships and properties of numbers or shapes; investigate a statement involving numbers and test it with examples.	
11. Hit the target		**Use/apply strand:** Solve one-step and two-step problems involving numbers, money or measures, including time; choose and carry out appropriate calculations. **Knowledge strand:** Derive and recall multiplication facts up to 10 × 10, the corresponding division facts and multiples of numbers to 10 up to the tenth multiple.	
12. Fraction dominoes		**Use/apply strand:** Represent a problem, using number sentences, statements or diagrams; use these to solve the problem; present and interpret the solution in the context of the problem. **Knowledge strand:** Identify pairs of fractions that total 1.	

Title of lesson	Year 3 objectives	Year 4 objectives	Tracking forward Year 5 objectives
13. Snack bar		**Knowledge strand:** Use knowledge of addition and subtraction facts and place value to derive sums and differences of pairs of multiples of 10.	**Use/apply strand:** Solve one-step and two-step problems involving whole numbers and decimals and all four operations, choosing and using appropriate methods, including calculator use.
14. Give and take	**Knowledge strand:** Use knowledge of number operations and corresponding inverses to check calculations.	**Use/apply strand:** Identify and use patterns, relationships and properties of numbers or shapes; investigate a statement involving numbers and test it with examples.	
15. Perfect numbers		**Use/apply strand:** Identify and use patterns, relationships and properties of numbers or shapes; investigate a statement involving numbers and test it with examples.	**Knowledge strand:** Identify pairs of factors of two-digit whole numbers and find common multiples (for example, for 6 and 9).
16. Number triplets	**Calculate strand:** Add or subtract mentally combinations of one-digit and two-digit numbers.	**Use/apply strand:** Identify and use patterns, relationships and properties of numbers or shapes; investigate a statement involving numbers and test it with examples.	
17. 20 up	**Calculate strand:** Add or subtract mentally combinations of one-digit and two-digit numbers.	**Use/apply strand:** Identify and use patterns, relationships and properties of numbers or shapes; investigate a statement involving numbers and test it with examples.	
18. Connections	**Calculate strand:** Add or subtract mentally combinations of one-digit and two-digit numbers.	**Use/apply strand:** Report solutions to problems, giving explanations and reasoning orally and in writing.	
19. Magic triangles	**Calculate strand:** Add or subtract mentally combinations of one-digit and two-digit numbers.	**Use/apply strand:** Report solutions to problems, giving explanations and reasoning orally and in writing.	
20. Crossovers		**Use/apply strand:** Identify and use patterns, relationships and properties of numbers or shapes; investigate a statement involving numbers and test it with examples. **Use/apply strand:** Report solutions to problems, giving explanations and reasoning orally and in writing.	
21. Intersections		**Use/apply strand:** Identify and use patterns, relationships and properties of numbers or shapes; investigate a statement involving numbers and test it with examples. **Use/apply strand:** Report solutions to problems, giving explanations and reasoning orally and in writing.	
22. Stars and moons	**Calculate strand:** Add or subtract mentally combinations of one-digit numbers.	**Use/apply strand:** Identify and use patterns, relationships and properties of numbers or shapes; investigate a statement involving numbers and test it with examples.	
23. Money exchange	**Calculate strand:** Add or subtract mentally combinations of one-digit and two-digit numbers.	**Use/apply strand:** Identify and use patterns, relationships and properties of numbers or shapes; investigate a statement involving numbers and test it with examples.	
24. In the balance	**Calculate strand:** Add or subtract mentally combinations of one-digit and two-digit numbers.	**Use/apply strand:** Represent a problem using number sentences and diagrams; use these to solve the problem; present and interpret the solution in the context of the problem.	
25. Missing numbers	**Calculate strand:** Add or subtract mentally combinations of one-digit and two-digit numbers.	**Use/apply strand:** Represent a problem using number sentences and diagrams; use these to solve the problem; present and interpret the solution in the context of the problem.	
26. Magic circles		**Use/apply strand:** Identify and use patterns, relationships and properties of numbers or shapes; investigate a statement involving numbers and test it with examples. **Use/apply strand:** Report solutions to problems, giving explanations and reasoning orally in writing. **Calculate strand:** Add or subtract mentally pairs of two-digit whole numbers (for example, 47 + 58, 91 – 35).	

Title of lesson	Year 3 objectives	Year 4 objectives	Tracking forward Year 5 objectives
27. Shrinking squares		**Use/apply strand:** Identify and use patterns, relationships and properties of numbers or shapes; investigate a statement involving numbers and test it with examples. **Calculate strand:** Subtract mentally pairs of two-digit whole numbers (for example, 91 – 35).	
28. Words worth		**Use/apply strand:** Collect, organise and interpret selected information to find answers. **Calculate strand:** Add or subtract mentally pairs of two-digit whole numbers (for example, 47 + 58, 91 – 35).	
29. Magic arc		**Use/apply strand:** Identify and use patterns, relationships and properties of numbers or shapes; investigate a statement involving numbers and test it with examples. **Use/apply strand:** Report solutions to problems, giving explanations and reasoning orally and in writing. **Calculate strand:** Add or subtract mentally pairs of two-digit whole numbers (for example, 47 + 58, 91 – 35).	
30. Bits and pieces		**Use/apply strand:** Solve one-step and two-step problems involving numbers, money or measures, including time; choose and carry out appropriate calculations. **Calculate strand:** Find fractions of numbers, quantities or shapes (for example, $1/5$ of 50 plums, $3/8$ of a 6 by 4 rectangle).	
31. Maze	**Shape strand:** Read and record the vocabulary of position, direction and movement, using the four compass directions to describe movement about a grid.	**Use/apply strand:** Report solutions to problems, giving explanations and reasoning orally and in writing.	
32. Triangle puzzle		**Use/apply strand:** Identify and use patterns, relationships and properties of numbers or shapes. **Shape strand:** Draw polygons and classify them by identifying their properties.	
33. Tangram puzzle		**Use/apply strand:** Identify and use patterns, relationships and properties of numbers or shapes. **Shape strand:** Draw polygons and classify them by identifying their properties.	
34. Robots	**Use/apply strand:** Represent the information in a problem, using numbers, images or diagrams; use these to find a solution and present it in context.	**Shape strand:** Visualise 3D objects from 2D drawings; make nets of common solids.	
35. Make that shape		**Use/apply strand:** Suggest a line of enquiry and the strategy needed to follow it; collect, organise and interpret selected information to find answers.	**Shape strand:** Use knowledge of properties to draw 2D shapes. **Shape strand:** Estimate, draw and measure acute and obtuse angles, using an angle measurer or protractor to a suitable degree of accuracy; calculate angles in a straight line.
36. 2D shape match		**Use/apply strand:** Identify and use patterns, relationships and properties of numbers or shapes; investigate a statement involving numbers and test it with examples. **Shape strand:** Draw polygons and classify them by identifying their properties.	
37. 3D shape match		**Use/apply strand:** Identify and use patterns, relationships and properties of numbers or shapes. **Shape strand:** Draw polygons and classify them by identifying their properties.	
38. What's in a shape?		**Use/apply strand:** Suggest a line of enquiry and the strategy needed to follow it; collect, organise and interpret selected information to find answers. **Use/apply strand:** Identify and use patterns, relationships and properties of numbers or shapes; investigate a statement involving numbers and test it with examples.	**Shape strand:** Identify, visualise and describe properties of rectangles, triangles, regular polygons and 3D solids.

PNS OBJECTIVES

Title of lesson	Year 3 objectives	Year 4 objectives	Tracking forward Year 5 objectives
39. On reflection	**Shape strand:** Draw and complete shapes with reflective symmetry; draw the reflection of a shape in a mirror line along one side.	**Use/apply strand:** Represent a problem, using number sentences, statements or diagrams; use these to solve the problem; present and interpret the solution in the context of the problem.	
40. Take five cubes	**Shape strand:** Relate 2D shapes and 3D solids to drawings of them; describe, visualise, classify, draw and make the shapes.	**Use/apply strand:** Represent a problem, using number sentences, statements or diagrams; use these to solve the problem; present and interpret the solution in the context of the problem.	
41. Scaled down		**Use/apply strand:** Suggest a line of enquiry and the strategy needed to follow it; collect, organise and interpret selected information to find answers. **Measure strand:** Choose and use standard metric units and their abbreviations when estimating, measuring and recording length, weight and capacity.	
42. Round the block		**Use/apply strand:** Suggest a line of enquiry and the strategy needed to follow it; collect, organise and interpret selected information to find answers. **Measure strand:** Draw rectangles and measure and calculate their perimeters; find the area of rectilinear shapes drawn on a square grid by counting squares.	
43. Measure for measure			**Use/apply strand:** Plan and pursue an enquiry; present evidence by collecting, organising and interpreting information. **Measure strand:** Read, choose, use and record standard metric units to estimate and measure length, weight and capacity; convert larger units to smaller units, using decimals to one place (for example, change 2.6kg to 2600g).
44. Time for mathematics		**Use/apply strand:** Solve one-step and two-step problems involving numbers, money or measures, including time; choose and carry out appropriate calculations. **Measure strand:** Read time to the nearest minute; use am, pm and 12-hour clock notation; calculate time intervals from clocks and timetables.	
45. Made to measure		**Use/apply strand:** Suggest a line of enquiry and the strategy needed to follow it; collect, organise and interpret selected information to find answers.	**Measure strand:** Read, choose, use and record standard metric units to estimate and measure length, weight and capacity to a suitable degree of accuracy (for example, the nearest centimetre).
46. Flags	**Data strand:** Answer a question by collecting, organising and interpreting data.	**Use/apply strand:** Suggest a line of enquiry and the strategy needed to follow it; collect, organise and interpret selected information to find answers.	
47. My day		**Use/apply strand:** Report solutions to problems, giving explanations and reasoning orally and in writing. **Data strand:** Answer a question by identifying what data to collect; organise, present, analyse and interpret the data in tables, diagrams, tally charts, pictograms and bar charts, using ICT where appropriate.	
48. Out for six	**Use/apply strand:** Follow a line of enquiry by deciding what information is important; make and use lists, tables and graphs to organise and interpret the information.		**Data strand:** Describe the occurrence of familiar events, using the language of chance or likelihood.
49. Double dice	**Knowledge strand:** Derive and recall all addition and subtraction facts for each number to 20.		**Data strand:** Describe the occurrence of familiar events, using the language of chance or likelihood.
50. Dice mix	**Knowledge strand:** Derive and recall multiplication facts for the 2, 3, 4, 5, 6 and 10 times-tables and the corresponding division facts.		**Data strand:** Describe the occurrence of familiar events, using the language of chance or likelihood.

SELF-ASSESSMENT ▢ RECORDING SHEET

Name: _____ Date: _____

Activity title:			
I can _____ _____ _____ _____ _____	 👍	 ✊	 👎
I was able to _____ _____ _____ _____ _____	 👍	 ✊	 👎

I can

_____

_____

_____

	Use/apply strand	Counting strand	Knowledge strand	Calculate strand	Shape strand	Measure strand	Data strand
1. Number generator	●	●					
2. Hidden answers	●		●				
3. Halfway there	●		●				
4. Puzzle corner	●		●				
5. Number hunt	●		●				
6. Cashing up	●			●			
7. That's odd	●			●			
8. Just 19	●			●			
9. Full to the brim	●			●			
10. Shape mix	●			●			
11. Target 34	●			●			
12. Age gap	●			●			
13. My perfect number	●			●			
14. Numbers up	●			●			
15. Chocolate selection	●			●			
16. What's in a name?	●				●		
17. Made to measure	●					●	
18. Something about me	●					●	
19. In the mix	●						●
20. Seeing spots	●						●

Brainteasers

1 Number generator

Thinking skills: Systematic and logical processes.

What to do: Read through the challenge (see photocopiable page 18) with the group or child and ensure they understand the objective of the task.

Probing questions: How will you begin? Are there more three-digit numbers? What is the value of the middle digit in that number?

Outcomes: Individuals may start in a fairly chaotic manner. To find all the possible ways it is helpful to list the solutions in a systematic way. There are 24 possible three-digit numbers. Looking at those featuring the digits 1, 2 and 3, the solutions are: 123, 132, 213, 231, 312, 321. Similar families will be generated using 1, 2, 4; 1, 3, 4 and 2, 3, 4.

Next steps: Change the digits (for example, to 3, 6, 8, 9) and consider recording the answers on a large (ungraduated) 0–1000 number line.

Learning objectives
(Y3) Counting strand: Read, write and order whole numbers to at least 1000 and position them on a number line.
(Y4) Use/apply strand: Suggest a line of enquiry and the strategy needed to follow it; collect, organise and interpret selected information to find answers.

2 Hidden answers

Thinking skills: Reasoning and logical processes.

What to do: Children may think that the task involves three separate questions: clarify from the outset that it does not. Encourage them to talk about possible strategies for tackling the problem before they begin.

Probing questions: How will you start? What numbers will you try first? Is that too much/too little?

Outcomes: The correct solution is 37p. One possible strategy is to develop three lists of possible answers based on the remainders of each of the multiples. Within the upper limit of 50p, there is just one satisfactory answer.

Learning objectives
(Y4) Use/apply strand: Represent a problem, using number sentences and diagrams; use these to solve the problem; present and interpret the solution in the context of the problem.
(Y4) Knowledge strand: Derive and recall multiplication facts up to 10 × 10, the corresponding division facts and multiples of numbers to 10 up to the tenth multiple.

Next steps: Create similar problems by choosing a number at random and identifying the remainder for a selection of different multiples. You may want to concentrate on multiples which the group are trying to learn 'by heart' at the present time.

3 Halfway there

Thinking skills: Logic and reasoning.

What to do: The question on page 19 deliberately avoids suggesting any strategy for solving the problem, so discuss different approaches before encouraging the children to tackle the problem themselves.

Probing questions: What will you do first to find the number that is halfway? What is your estimate of the answer? Is there another way of calculating the answer? (The solution is 54.)

Outcomes: Once a satisfactory approach and solution has been reached, the different methods can be compared. This task offers a potential introduction to the idea of averages (mean).

Next steps: Set the range more widely or provide numbers which lead to a mid-point halfway between two adjacent whole numbers.

> **Learning objectives**
> **(Y4) Use/apply strand:** Solve one-step and two-step problems involving numbers, money or measures; choose and carry out appropriate calculations.
> **(Y4) Knowledge strand:** Use knowledge of rounding, number operations and inverses to check calculations.

4 Puzzle corner

Thinking skill: Reasoning.

What to do: Ensure that the group are comfortable with the terms 'difference' and 'product'.

Probing questions: How will you begin to tackle these puzzles? What information do you have? What operations did you use?

Outcomes: The complexity of language will be one of the principal challenges of these two tasks. As with many of these types of problems, a typical strategy is to begin by listing all possible combinations for one of the conditions. The solutions are 53 and 27, and 8 and 3.

Next steps: Set similar problems in real contexts (for example, rework the featured 'totals and differences' problem in terms of finding the ages of two people).

> **Learning objectives**
> **(Y4) Use/apply strand:** Suggest a line of enquiry and the strategy needed to follow it; collect, organise and interpret selected information to find answers.
> **(Y4) Knowledge strand:** Use knowledge of rounding, number operations and inverses to check calculations.

5 Number hunt

Thinking skills: Reasoning and systematic working.

What to do: Ensure that the children are comfortable with the concept of division with/without remainders.

Probing questions: How are you going to tackle the problem? Do you think that the answer will be an even number? What digits do multiples of 5 have at the end?

Outcomes: Individuals may approach this by listing multiples of some or all of the featured factors. Some may even have an intuitive sense of the type of number which is likely to have several factors.

Solution: The lowest common factor, and the only such two-digit number, is 60.

Next steps: Provide similar tasks using a different combination of factors.

> **Learning objectives**
> **(Y4) Use/apply strand:** Suggest a line of enquiry and the strategy needed to follow it; collect, organise and interpret selected information to find answers.
> **(Y5) Knowledge strand:** Identify pairs of factors of two-digit whole numbers and find common multiples (such as for 6 and 9).

Learning objectives
(Y3) Calculate strand: Add or subtract mentally combinations of one-digit and two-digit numbers.
(Y4) Use/apply strand: Represent a problem, using number sentences and diagrams; use these to solve the problem; present and interpret the solution in the context of the problem.

6 Cashing up

Thinking skills: Logical and systematic processes.

What to do: Encourage the children to think about and discuss strategies. You could suggest a systematic strategy (see table right) to find all the coin combinations.

Probing questions: How will you start? What coin will you start with next? Have you found all the different ways to make 14p?

Outcomes: Numerically the task is not too challenging as the target total is relatively small. The real complexity comes from having to establish an exhaustive strategy that best ensures no coin combinations are overlooked. There are 16 unique combinations: the table shows the number of each type of coin.

5p	2p	1p
0	0	14
0	1	12
0	2	10
0	3	8
0	4	6
0	5	4
0	6	2
0	7	0
1	0	9
1	1	7
1	2	5
1	3	3
1	4	1
2	0	4
2	1	2
2	2	0

Next steps: Change the target total and/or the range of coin denominations available. Set other coin problems where there might be more than one answer (for example, make 50p using six coins).

Learning objectives
(Y3) Calculate strand: Add or subtract mentally combinations of one-digit and two-digit numbers.
(Y4) Use/apply strand: Suggest a line of enquiry and the strategy needed to follow it; collect, organise and interpret selected information to find answers.

7 That's odd

Thinking skills: Logical and systematic processes.

What to do: Explain to the children that they can use the same number twice in their addition. Discuss possible strategies - for example, subtracting odd numbers from 24.

Probing questions: What is the largest odd number you can use? What number will you start with next? Have you found them all?

Outcomes: This task has several answers - for example, 21 + 1 + 1 + 1, 17 + 1 + 3 + 3, 15 + 1 + 3 + 5 and 3 + 5 + 7 + 9. The task is made more comprehensive by asking the group to try to find all possible answers. (I have found 24 uniquely different combinations.)

Next steps: Increase or reduce the target total and consider using even numbers only. Create a real context by setting a target total to be made with a limited range of coin denominations.

Learning objectives
(Y3) Calculate strand: Add or subtract mentally combinations of one-digit and two-digit numbers.
(Y4) Use/apply strand: Solve one-step and two-step problems involving numbers, money or measures; choose and carry out appropriate calculations.

8 Just 19

Thinking skills: Number manipulation and calculation.

What to do: Read the challenge on page 21 with the child or group and check that they understand the mathematical terms. If necessary, set a couple of target numbers to confirm that they appreciate what the task demands.

Probing questions: How did you work out that total? Which number did you use first? Is there another way? What will you try next?

Outcomes: It is possible to create a number sentence for every counting number in the given range. In some cases there will be more than one way. Check that every given number sentence is correct, and use subtly different number sentences to contrast and compare (for example, 9 - 2 + 8 gives the same result as 9 + 8 - 2).

Next steps: Consider working with a different set of numbers or extend the target range by allowing any combination of the four operations.

Learning objectives
(Y3) Calculate strand: Add or subtract mentally combinations of one-digit and two-digit numbers.
(Y4) Use/apply strand: Represent a problem, using number sentences and diagrams; use these to solve the problem; present and interpret the solution in the context of the problem.

9 Full to the brim

Thinking skills: Information processing and reasoning.

What to do: The task presented on page 22 offers potential for communicating strategies and solutions. The idea of filling 'to the brim' may represent unfamiliar language, so ensure that the children understand the aim of the task before they tackle it independently.

Probing questions: What strategies could you try first? How do you know that will work? Can you explain that another way?

Outcomes: To measure 2 units of water you first need to fill the 5 unit jug from the tap. This can then be used to fill the 3 unit jug to the brim, leaving 2 units of water in the larger jug, which can be poured into the bowl. To measure 1 unit of water, the 3 unit jug is filled from the tap and emptied into the 5 unit jug. The 3 unit jug is then re-filled from the tap and used to 'top up' the 5 unit jug to capacity. The smaller jug now holds 1 unit of water.

Next steps: Ask the group to explore what measurements can be made with 3 and 7 unit capacity jugs.

Learning objectives
(Y3) Calculate strand: Add or subtract mentally combinations of one-digit and two-digit numbers.
(Y4) Use/apply strand: Represent a problem, using number sentences and diagrams; use these to find a strategy to solve the problem and present the solution in the context of the problem.

10 Shape mix

Thinking skills: Logical and systematic processes.

What to do: Ensure the children understand that the aim of the task on page 22 is to add the numbers of sides of each shape to make a total of 15. Although the task appears to be a shape activity, the mathematics is essentially based around the use of the numbers 3, 4 and 5 to make a total of 15.

Probing questions: How will you start? What addition will you try next? Have you found all the ways of making a total of 15?

Outcomes: Some children might sketch their ideas on individual whiteboards while others may spontaneously convert the task into an exclusively number-based problem, thus avoiding the drawing of shapes. The solutions (based on the initial letters of shapes) are as follows:

T, T, T, T, T   S, S, S, T   P, P, P   P, S, T, T

Next steps: Change the mix and range of shapes permitted and/or the target number of sides.

Learning objectives
(Y3) Calculate strand: Add or subtract mentally combinations of one-digit and two-digit numbers.
(Y4) Use/apply strand: Suggest a line of enquiry and the strategy needed to follow it; collect, organise and interpret selected information to find answers.

11 Target 34

Thinking skills: Enquiry and calculation.

What to do: You may need to clarify the word 'consecutive' before the children attempt the task presented on page 23. You could also talk about the possible strategies they could use.

Probing questions: What does the word 'consecutive' mean? What numbers and operations will you try first? Is there another way to reach the total?

Outcomes: There are three solutions to the task: $4 + 5 \times 6$, $6 \times 7 - 8$ and $35 + 36 - 37$. Brackets are not required in either case because, in their absence, multiplication takes precedence over addition.

Next steps: Create similar problems, asking the children to find three consecutive numbers with a total of 45, four even numbers with a total of 20, or two numbers with a difference of 10 and a product of 24.

Learning objectives
(Y4) Use/apply strand: Solve one-step and two-step problems involving numbers, money or measures; choose and carry out appropriate calculations.
(Y4) Calculate strand: Add or subtract mentally pairs of two-digit whole numbers (such as 47 + 58, 91 – 35).

12 Age gap

Thinking skill: Reasoning.

What to do: Ensure the children understand the task outlined on page 23. Discuss various strategies for solving the problem before they tackle it independently.

Probing questions: How will you begin to solve this problem? What information do you know? What operations might you use?

Outcomes: The most typical strategy is either to find all the age combinations with a difference of 16 or to write a list of numbers and their triples. Scrutiny of either one of these lists will identify a unique combination where both conditions are simultaneously satisfied. In the task presented on page 23, the correct combination of ages is 24 and 8 years; Jodie is 8.

Next steps: Ask the children to consider their own situation, identifying how old they will be in the future in relation to other family members. If it is not considered too sensitive, ask group members to think about when they will be exactly half the age of their mothers.

Learning objectives
(Y4) Use/apply strand: Solve one-step and two-step problems involving numbers, money or measures; choose and carry out appropriate calculations.
(Y4) Calculate strand: Find fractions of numbers, quantities or shapes, (such as $^1/_5$ of 30 plums, $^3/_8$ of a 6 by 4 rectangle).

13 My perfect number

Thinking skills: Calculation and reasoning.

What to do: Depending on the abilities of the children, an introductory session on the mathematical operations involved may be necessary. For example, you may want to establish why 50% of 8 and 25% of 16 are both equivalent to 4. Concentrate on the way that one calculation can often lead to another related fact (such as the 'doubling and halving' in the example above).

Probing questions: Can you make a similar number sentence using different numbers? What other operation could you try? Could you use fractions?

Outcomes: The complexity of the task will depend on the extent to which children are encouraged to be adventurous in their choice of mathematics.

Next steps: Allow the use of two-digit or three-digit numbers.

Learning objectives
(Y4) Use/apply strand: Report solutions to problems, giving explanations and reasoning orally and in writing.
(Y4) Calculate strand: Add or subtract mentally pairs of two-digit whole numbers (such as 47 + 58, 91 – 35).

14 Numbers up

Thinking skills: Selecting and reasoning.

What to do: Discuss a range of strategies for the mental addition of numbers.

Probing questions: Which card will you choose first? How did you find that total? Can you add the cards in a different order?

Outcomes: As the numbers on the cards are all powers of 2, they can be used to make every two-digit number. Try to establish the range of calculation strategies and encourage techniques such as making progressive use of the largest available numbers.

Next steps: If the cards are presented in descending order as column headings within a table, any given target number can be recorded as a combination of 1s and 0s. This provides the basis for the binary system (which is fundamental to the operation of computer systems and a whole host of other electronic devices).

Learning objectives
(Y4) Use/apply strand:
Represent a problem, using number sentences and diagrams; use these to solve the problem; present and interpret the solution in the context of the problem.
(Y5) Calculate strand: Extend mental methods for whole-number calculations, for example to multiply a two-digit by a one-digit number, to multiply by 25, to subtract one near-multiple of 1000 from another.

15 Chocolate selection

Thinking skills: Interpreting information and finding strategies.

What to do: Explain to the children the aim of the task on page 25 and encourage them to discuss their ideas for tackling the problem. Ensure they understand the need to use multiplication to find the answer.

Probing questions: How will you start to tackle the problem? What numbers will you try first? Is that total too little/too much?

Outcomes: Although the problem could be solved algebraically using simultaneous equations ($10a + 5b = 120$ and $a + b = 20$), it is more realistic to adopt a 'trial and improvement' strategy. The correct solution is $16 \times 5p$ and $4 \times 10p$.

Next steps: Change the context to other real-life situations. For example, ask the children to work out how many cars and motorbikes there are in a car park if there is a total of ten vehicles and you can count a total of 34 wheels.

Learning objectives
(Y4) Use/apply strand:
Represent a problem, using number sentences and diagrams; use these to solve the problem; present and interpret the solution in the context of the problem.
(Y4) Shape strand: Draw polygons and classify them by identifying their properties.

16 What's in a name?

Thinking skills: Enquiry and information processing.

What to do: Provide mathematical dictionaries or other reference texts to support the children in the task. You might also encourage individuals to find the required information using an internet search engine.

Probing questions: How many vertices does your shape have? Can you think of another shape with four sides? How could we find out the name for this shape? What do you notice about the endings of lots of these words?

Outcomes: Observe the children's drawings of the shapes and ask questions to identify whether the irregular representations are considered as much as the more familiar, regular versions (such as a square or a kite shape). Encourage the children to consider how the words are 'built', often with the ending of '-agon' meaning '-sided shape'.

Next steps: Extend the number of shapes to include those with 11 and 12 sides. You could also investigate all the different types of four-sided shapes (quadrilaterals).

Learning objectives
(Y4) Use/apply strand: Report solutions to problems, giving explanations and reasoning orally and in writing.
(Y4) Measure strand: Choose and use standard metric units and their abbreviations when estimating, measuring and recording length, weight and capacity; know the meaning of 'kilo', 'centi' and 'milli' and, where appropriate, use decimal notation to record measurements (such as 1.3m or 0.6kg).

17 Made to measure

Thinking skills: Processing information and making choices.

What to do: Ensure the children understand the different units of measurement used for liquids, solids and length. Encourage them to experiment with measuring jugs, tape measures and scales to confirm their understanding.

Probing questions: What units might we use when measuring liquids? What does 'g' stand for on this food label? What measuring instrument would we use for finding the length of the school field?

Outcomes: This is a fairly open task involving the compilation of lists. Consider the appropriateness of the items chosen. Where smaller/larger units would be more appropriate (for example, millilitres), establish whether the children are familiar with these.

Next steps: Extend the task to include imperial measures (for example, miles and pints).

18 Something about me

Thinking skills: Processing information and making creative choices.

What to do: Provide weighing scales and tape measures for the activity on page 26. Encourage the children to think of possible personal facts that involve numbers: their mass, height, distance they live from school, arm length and so on.

Probing questions: How many months are there in a year? What units do we use for measuring mass? What measuring equipment would you like to use?

Outcomes: This activity tends towards a measurement task but you might also focus on more random statistics (for example, house numbers).

Next steps: Refine the level of accuracy required by the task (for example, children could estimate their age in minutes or seconds); make use of calculators as required.

19 In the mix

Thinking skills: Logical and systematic processes, processing data.

What to do: Demonstrate to the children the process of throwing the dice and multiplying the two resulting numbers together (for example, $2 \times 4 = 8$). Explain that they will need to write down each multiplication sentence and answer.

Probing questions: How did you calculate that answer? Is there another way of getting that answer? Which outcome is most likely?

Outcomes: Identify all the possible outcomes by listing each product in a probability space (see right). Within this there are 18 different answers.

×	1	2	3	4	5	6
1	1	2	3	4	5	6
2	2	4	6	8	10	12
3	3	6	9	12	15	18
4	4	8	12	16	20	24
5	5	10	15	20	25	30
6	6	12	18	24	30	36

Next steps: Use the information gathered in the table to identify which numbers are more likely to be scored when the numbers on the dice are multiplied together. Begin to quantify these as a fractional amount (for example, the probability of scoring 12 is $^4/_{36}$, or $^1/_9$).

20 Seeing spots

Thinking skills: Systematic and logical processes.

What to do: Make sure the children understand the activity – perhaps by identifying one of the possible methods before they start.

Probing questions: How will you start? What will you change? Have you found all the combinations?

Outcomes: There are 16 different ways: 1 way with no blanks, 4 ways with one blank, 6 ways with two blanks, 4 ways with three blanks and 1 way with four blanks. Focus attention on the symmetry of these answers, noting how each arrangement has its own opposite (inverse).

Next steps: The task can be modelled with a block of four interlocking cubes using two colours only. Explore real-life contexts: for example, consider how many different outfits are possible if you have two hats, three tops and two pairs of shorts to choose from.

1: Number generator

◖ Make three-digit numbers using these cards (for example, 314).

1	2	3	4

◖ Have you found them all?
◖ Now put them in order.

2: Hidden answers

◖ I have less than 50p.

◖ If I share the money between four people I have 1p left over.
◖ If I share the money between five people I have 2p left over.
◖ If I share the money between six people I have 1p left over.

◖ How much do I have?

_____

_____

3: Halfway there

■ What number is halfway between 12 and 96?

■ Now choose some two-digit numbers of your own and find out which number is halfway between them.

■ How did you work out the middle number?

✂ -

4: Puzzle corner

■ Find two whole numbers with a sum of 80 and a difference of 26.

■ Find two whole numbers with a sum of 11 and a product of 24.

■ Now make your own puzzles like this but change the numbers.

5: Number hunt

■ Find a two-digit number that can be divided by 1, 2, 3, 4, 5 and 6 without a remainder.

6: Cashing up

■ Find the different ways of making 14p using only 5p, 2p and 1p coins.

PHOTOCOPIABLE **■SCHOLASTIC**
www.scholastic.co.uk

7: That's odd

■ Find any four odd numbers with a total of 24.

1	2	3	4	5	6	7	8
9	10	11	12	13	14	15	16
17	18	19	20	21	22	23	24

■ Can you find more odd numbers with the same total of 24?

8: Just 19

9	8
7	2

■ Using some or all of these numbers each time, can you make every counting number from 1 to 19 using only addition and/or subtraction? For example, 4 is made with the number sentence 9 – 7 + 2.

9: Full to the brim

■ These two jugs have no scale to measure smaller amounts of water.

■ How would you use them to pour 2 units of water into the bowl?

■ How would you use the two jugs to measure 1 unit of water?

10: Shape mix

■ Collect a total of 15 sides using some or all of these shapes.

■ Can you find a different combination of these shapes? Each shape can be used any number of times in each answer.

11: Target 34

■ Find three consecutive numbers which can be combined to make 34. You can use the operations +, −, × and ÷, but you can use each digit only once.

■ There is more than one way to make 34. Can you find another?

12: Age gap

■ Matt is three times older than Jodie and their age difference is 16 years. How old is Jodie?

13: My perfect number

◄ Choose your favourite single-digit number and make 20 number sentences with that answer.
◄ Use addition, subtraction, multiplication, division, fractions and percentages in your number sentences.

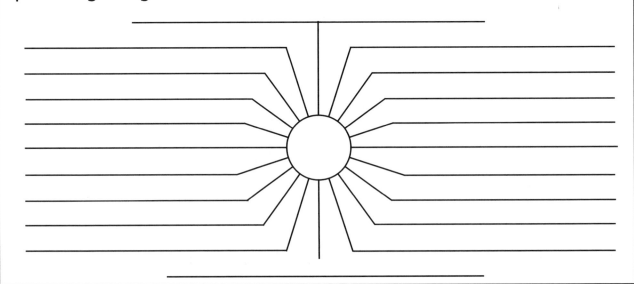

14: Numbers up

◄ Choose any two-digit target number.
◄ Use two or more of these number cards to make your chosen number (for example, 51 = 16 + 32 + 2 + 1).
◄ You may only add the numbers.
◄ Each number card may only be used once.

8	4	32	64	16	2	1

PHOTOCOPIABLE **SCHOLASTIC**
www.scholastic.co.uk

15: Chocolate selection

◢ Twenty chocolates are priced individually at 10p and 5p. If their total cost is £1.20, how many of each chocolate will you have?

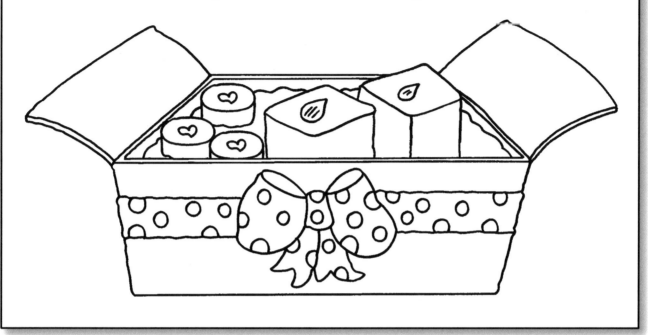

16: What's in a name?

◢ Draw and name 2D shapes with 3, 4, 5, 6, 7, 8, 9 and 10 sides.

◢ Do you know the names of 3D shapes with 4, 5, 6, 8 and 12 faces too?

17: Made to measure

■ Make lists of things you might measure
in litres, metres and kilograms.

litres	metres	kilograms

✂ -

18: Something about me

■ Think of and write a list
of facts about yourself
where all the answers are
numbers.
■ Think about things such
as your age in months,
your height, your mass
and your favourite number.

PHOTOCOPIABLE **SCHOLASTIC**
www.scholastic.co.uk

19: In the mix

◖ Throw two dice and multiply the numbers on each dice together.

◖ How many different answers are possible?

20: Seeing spots

◖ This square has four spots. The spots can be shaded or blank as in this example.

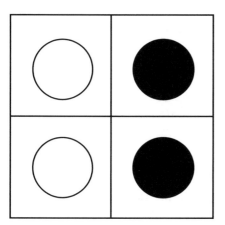

◖ Find different ways of shading and not shading four spots arranged as a square.

◖ Have you found them all?

Nearest ten

Learning objectives
(Y3) Use/apply strand:
Follow a line of enquiry by deciding what information is important.
(Y3) Counting strand:
Round two-digit or three-digit numbers to the nearest 10.

Expected prior knowledge
● As the idea of rounding is developed in the lesson introduction, there are no specific pre-requisites for this activity.

You will need
Large demonstration number line; photocopiable page 29 (one per child); standard dice (two per pair or small group of up to four children); counters (seven per child).

Key vocabulary
round up/down, nearest multiple of 10, rule (in the sense of rounding conventions), probability, likelihood

Brainteaser link
1: 'Number generator' on page 11.

Activity introduction
● Use a large demonstration number line to highlight the multiples of 10 from 0 to 100. Identify any two-digit number and discuss the idea of 'the nearest multiple of 10'.
● You could relate this strategy to work the class may have done on counting on from one number to another, using the multiple of 10 as a 'bridging point'.
● Explore other two-digit numbers, including one ending with the digit 5, to highlight the convention of rounding up even though there is not strictly a 'nearest multiple of 10'.
● Discuss the need to use rounding up or rounding down to give an approximation of a number, perhaps in cases where the exact value is not critical. This idea is developed more fully in the Review session.
● Ask questions: *What is the nearest multiple of 10? Will you round up or down? How close is this number to the nearest multiple of 10?*

Activity development
● Provide each child with photocopiable page 29. Arrange the children into pairs or small groups. Give each pair or group two standard dice (numerals are preferable to spots but not essential) and some counters. Explain the rules (as follows) and, as they play, encourage the children to ask each other questions as detailed in the lesson introduction.
● Players take turns to roll two dice. From these two dice a number is created (for example, a 1 and a 6 can be used to create either 16 or 61).
● The player must then round that number to the nearest multiple of 10. If that multiple of 10 is still available to the player, they cover that number on their sheet with a counter.
● The winner is the first player to cover all of the featured multiples on their sheet.

Review
● Review the game and look at aspects of likelihood. The target number 70, for example, can be achieved only by rounding up the dice combinations creating 65 or 66. As there are only two ways to secure a 6 and a 5, and just one way to score a double 6, the likelihood is relatively low.
● Demonstrate and discuss the concept of rounding in a practical context, such as money. By rounding two near multiples of 10, it is possible to get a rough idea of how much money to make available to the shopkeeper.

Next steps
● Investigate rounding to the nearest 100 or 1000. Talk about contexts where such approximations would be appropriate (for example, attendance figures at a major sporting event).
● Use rounding to the nearest 10 and then 'compensation' methods to calculate differences between any two numbers (for example, the difference between 38 and 82 is 4 more than the difference between 40 and 80).

Nearest ten

◼ You will need two dice, some counters and a friend to work with you.
◼ Use your knowledge of rounding up and down to play this game.

100% effort

Learning objectives
(Y4) Use/apply strand:
Solve one-step and two-step problems involving numbers, money or measures, including time; choose and carry out appropriate calculations.
(Y5) Counting strand:
Understand percentage as the number of parts in every 100 and express tenths and hundredths as percentages.

Expected prior knowledge
● Work with common percentages equivalent to one quarter, one half and three quarters.
● Recall or quickly derive multiplication facts up to 10 × 10.

You will need
Photocopiable page 31 (one per group).

Key vocabulary
fraction, multiplied by, percentage, equal parts, equals, method

Activity introduction
Write the number 20 in the centre of the board, radiate a line from it and write the statement '100% of 20'. Explain what 100% means in the context of a fraction. Radiate another arm from the number 20 and invite other statements with the same outcome, such as '50% of 40' and '200% of 10'.
● Ask questions: *What fraction is that percentage equivalent to? How did you work that out?*

Activity development
● The children can do this activity individually or in pairs. Prepare a set of cards (enlarged if possible) created from photocopiable page 31.
● Shuffle the pack of cards and share all of them around the group (some children may have more than one card).
● Ask one individual or pair to read out the question on their card and invite the group to calculate the answer.
● The numerical answer should be found at the top of one of the other cards, and it is from this card that the next question is drawn.
● If all the calculations are completed accurately, the last remaining card should feature a question which 'loops back' to the answer at the top of the card that was used to start the task.
● Try to establish both the answer and the strategy for calculation. Some children may adopt the techniques sampled in the lesson introduction, others may use their own methods.
● Ask questions: *How did you get that answer? What fraction is that percentage equivalent to? Does that answer seem reasonable?*
● Make use of the representations of the percentage on each card. Encourage the idea of estimation so that, when an answer is calculated, it is possible to establish whether the answer is reasonable.

Review
● Look at real-life contexts to see how well children apply their understanding of percentages. For example: Consider the cost of child-appropriate items in a 20% sale; Establish how many boys are in a class of 30 when 40% are girls.

Next steps
● Look for opportunities to apply these skills further through suitable data handling techniques (for example, using percentages in the creation of a pie chart).

100% effort

48	40	15	45	20
20% of 200	25% of 60	50% of 90	75% of 24	30% of 70
18	3	16	54	35
10% of 30	20% of 80	40% of 50	100% of 10	75% of 80
21	30	14	36	2
60% of 50	70% of 20	90% of 60	90% of 90	80% of 60
10	32	4	1	49
80% of 40	5% of 80	50% of 70	10% of 20	5% of 20
60	8	24	81	
10% of 80	75% of 32	60% of 60	70% of 70	

Code breaker

Activity introduction
● Provide each child with an individual whiteboard and ask them to draw three squares in a line (similar in layout to those shown on photocopiable page 33).
● Tell them that you are thinking of a secret number using the digits 7, 8 and 9. Ask them to write a three-digit number on this basis and ask related questions: *How do you say your number? What is the value of the middle digit? Is your number even? Can you round your number to the nearest 10 or 100? What is the largest number you can make using these digits?*
● Go around the group again, telling individuals whether their number is higher or lower than your secret number. Explain that they are allowed to use any one digit more than once. Continue to provide clues until the combination for the secret number is found.
● If time allows, play a similar game with a different set of digits.

Activity development
● Provide each child with photocopiable page 33, with the clue cards cut out from the lower panel. Stack the clue cards face down, ordered so that children read them in the correct order (the circles at the top indicate the order).
● Talk through the task outlined on the sheet, making sure that the idea of 'code breaking' is understood.
● Observe the children generating possible combinations of the three digits to create the code-breaking number, checking they appreciate that the same digit can be sampled more than once in a combination (333, for example) and noting those children who exhibit elements of systematic working (for example, 'locking' the first digit and rotating the other two options).
● Question the children again about their appreciation of place value within three-digit numbers.
● Ask them to look at their first clue card to help narrow down their search, observing those who readily interpret the mathematical language. At this stage you might suggest they strike out some of their codes. Use this refinement to gather a list of possible outcomes.
● The second and final clue cards can then be used to establish that the only feasible answer is 131.

Review
● Present a related task where systematic work is overtly taught. This might again involve finding three-digit codes using the digits 1, 2 and 3, this time with the constraint that each digit must be used in each combination. List all six outcomes and invite the children to find the same using an alternative approach. Look at the order within the six solutions (note that each digit leads the combination on two occasions).

> ### Next steps
> ● Look at all possible three-digit combinations made of the digits 1 and 2 only. (There are eight combinations: 1, 1, 1; 1, 2, 2; 2, 1, 2; 2, 2, 1; 1, 1, 2; 2, 1, 1; 1, 2, 1; 2, 2, 2.)

Code breaker

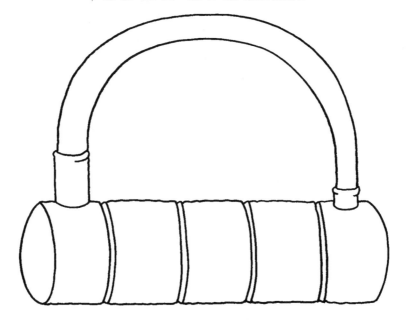

The code for this lock uses the digits 1, 2 and 3 only.

- Break the secret code.
- Remember, the same digit could be used more than once.

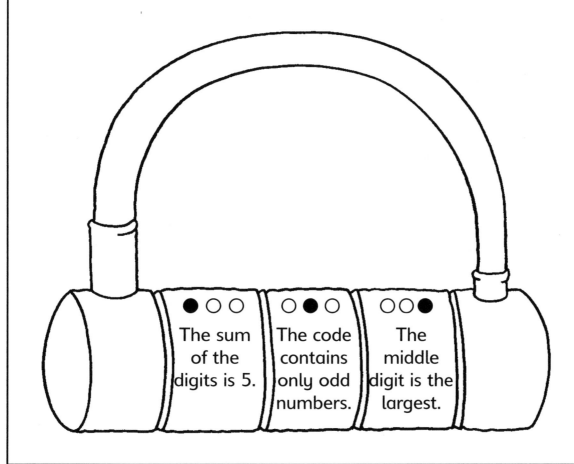

● ○ ○   ○ ● ○   ○ ○ ●

The sum of the digits is 5. | The code contains only odd numbers. | The middle digit is the largest.

All in proportion

Learning objectives
(Y4) Use/apply strand: Suggest a line of enquiry and the strategy needed to follow it; collect, organise and interpret selected information to find answers.
(Y5) Counting strand: Use sequences to scale numbers up or down; solve problems involving proportions of quantities (for example, decrease quantities in a recipe designed to feed six people).

Expected prior knowledge
● Use the common units for mass (g) and capacity (ml).

You will need
Photocopiable page 35 (one per child/pair); equipment for cooking (optional).

Key vocabulary
extra, more, less, ratio, proportion, amount, measure, scale, quantity

Activity introduction
● Look at a range of examples of scaling, targeting questions at individuals. For example: enlarging a rectangular playground by a factor of 2; spending an amount of money for four people then adjusting for more/fewer; buying bottles of drinks based on a calculation of 400ml per head.
● Ask questions: *How did you work out the answer? Is there another way? What units do we use for this measurement? What other units might we measure this in?*
● Introduce some of the key vocabulary (see left). For some children, the idea of ratio and proportion may not previously have been addressed directly.

Activity development
● Provide one copy of photocopiable page 35 per child or pair. Discuss the ingredients, covering their function (for example, sugar is a sweetener) and their unit of measure. Explain that the cake recipe is suitable only for a maximum of 8, while the party it is needed for has 12 children.
● Ask questions: *How many more people are coming? Is that twice as many? How many eggs would be needed in a cake for four?*
● If the concept of 'half as much again' is too complex at this stage, use the technique of reducing by half (for 4 people) before trebling (for 12 people). The quantities have all been set to provide convenient quantities when increased by 50%.
● Set the children working alone or in pairs, observing how they scale up each ingredient. If the task proves too challenging, the relative size of the cake can be set as a whole number multiple of the original (for example, double).

Review
● Further experience of scaling can be carried out practically with actual cooking activities.
● Look at the scales featured on measuring jugs, noting how some do not feature numerical readings alongside each marker. Talk about scales of differently sized graduations.
● Further work involving the reading of scales can be conducted using particular software (for example, Interactive Teaching Programmes).

Next steps
● Look at examples of scaling down (for example, the total cost of a trip shared between a number of family groups of different sizes).
● Consider word problems involving ratio (for example, ask: *In a class of 24, there were twice as many girls as boys. How many boys were in the class?*

All in proportion

■ What quantity of each ingredient is needed to make a cake for 12 people?

_____

_____

_____

_____

_____

_____

_____

Ingredients for a rich chocolate cake (serves 8):

1 teaspoon of bicarbonate of soda

50g cocoa powder

100g softened butter

2 large eggs

250ml milk

250g caster sugar

1 tablespoon of lemon juice

230g plain flour

Teacher's orders

Learning objectives
(Y4) Use/apply strand: Solve one-step and two-step problems involving numbers, money or measures; choose and carry out appropriate calculations.
(Y4) Counting strand: Use decimal notation for tenths and hundredths; relate the notation to money and measurement.

Expected prior knowledge
● Use money and record monetary amounts in pounds to two decimal places.
● Use a calculator (see Review).
● Use a large demonstration number line.

You will need
Large demonstration number line; photocopiable page 37 (one per pair/group); demonstration money; calculators.

Key vocabulary
factor, multiple, amount, calculate, total, sub-total, memory keys

Activity introduction
● Look at the factors of 30, as knowledge of these will be useful later in the lesson. The factors can be established by several different methods (grouping, for example). Model the task using a large demonstration number line showing 0 to 30, with jumps of a chosen step size from 0 (or back from 30).
● Ask questions: *Why do you think this number will be a factor of 30? What number fact would help you with that?*
● Establish that the factors of 30 are 1, 2, 3, 5, 6, 10, 15 and 30.
● Prepare the children fully with a real-life context of grouping by asking: *If a car can carry four children to school, how many cars would be needed to transport 30 children?* Four is not a factor of 30; the answer (7.5) needs in this context to be rounded up to 8, as the number of cars must be a whole number. Before moving on, ensure that this 'over-provision' is understood.

Activity development
● Provide each pair or group with a copy of photocopiable page 37. Review the sheet together and ensure that the children are clear that, in order to provide for the class of 30, they may sometimes need to purchase more than is immediately necessary.
● If the children have not had the experience of repeated addition (or multiplication) of amounts of money in £.p notation, it may be necessary to modify the sheet to more convenient quantities (rounded to the nearest multiple of 50p, for example) or simply to reduce the costs of each pack (so that each costs less than £1.00).
● You could provide money for calculation but the amounts given may make this impracticable within a group situation.
● Ask questions: *How many of each pack will you need? How will you work out the answer? What operation will you use for this? Does that seem a reasonable answer?*

Solution
● 5 sets of pencils, 3 sets of rulers, 2 sets of handwriting pens, 8 sets of pencil sharpeners:
£1.50 × 5 + £2.80 × 3 + £5.55 × 2 + £1.75 × 8 = £41.00.

Review
● Provide each group member with a calculator and demonstrate how two or more calculations can be completed in just one key sequence using the appropriate memory functions. For example, (3 × £5) + (6 × £4) is achieved by adding the £15 from the first calculation to the memory before adding the £24 similarly. (Refer to the user instructions if necessary, as the functionality of calculators can vary.)

Next steps
● Develop a party scenario (or other context) where multiple purchases are made. Alternatively, plan situations where items must be increased proportionately (for example, baking a cake for 12 from a recipe for 8).

Teacher's orders

Pencils
Pack of 6 for £1.50

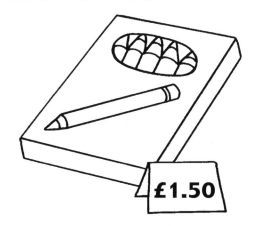

£1.50

Rulers
Value pack of 12 for £2.80

£2.80

Handwriting pens
Pack of 20 costs £5.55

£5.55

Pencil sharpeners
Saver pack of 4 for just £1.75

£1.75

◀ Use the information above to work out how much equipment a school needs to buy for a class of 30 children.

◀ How much will the total order cost the school?

_____

_____

_____

_____

Big car, little car

Learning objectives
(Y4) Use/apply strand:
Suggest a line of enquiry
and the strategy needed to
follow it; collect, organise
and interpret selected
information to find answers.
(Y4) Knowledge strand:
Derive and recall
multiplication facts up to
10×10.

Expected prior knowledge
● Generate multiples of
single-digit numbers.
● Add a pair of two-digit
numbers reliably.

You will need
Large 100-square; small
removable memo stickers;
photocopiable page 39 (one
per child/pair).

Key vocabulary
multiple, pattern,
combination, strategy

Brainteaser links
4: 'Puzzle corner' on page
12.
15: 'Chocolate selection' on
page 16.

Multiples of 5	Multiples of 8
5	8
10	16
15	24
20	32
25	40
30	
35	
40	

Activity introduction
● Present a large 100-square, explaining that you want to focus on
multiples of 8. Place a small sticker on 8 and another on 16, giving the
number sentence $8 \times 2 = 16$. Invite children to place stickers for the
next two multiples of 8, each time giving the appropriate number
sentence ($8 \times 3 = 24$ and $8 \times 4 = 32$).
● Turn attention to where multiples of 8 appear in the columns,
beginning by asking for a prediction of where the next multiple of 8
arises in the column containing 8. Do the same with the columns
containing 16 and 24 and then test out the predictions by counting on
in 8s from 32.
● Recap on knowledge of the 5 times table up to (and possibly beyond)
50, drawing attention to the fact that an even multiple of 5 has an
answer ending with the digit zero.

Activity development
● Provide each child or pair with photocopiable page 39, pointing out
the difference between large cars (sometimes called 'people-carriers')
and the more common hatchback/saloon vehicles.
● Clarify the expectation of the task. Explain that both types of car may
be used in tandem to reach the solution. Each car must be up to
capacity to qualify as being 'full' (8 people in the case of a large car, 5 in
a small one).
● Observe the way a solution is attempted. Some children may try to
work in multiples of 8 to approach the target total. Others may work up
from 5 in steps of that amount. Another strategy is simply to 'pick and
mix' combinations of vehicles and trial and improve until the solution is
reached.
● Ask questions: *How did you find the solution? Which totals between
40 and 50 cannot be made?*

Solution
● Four big cars and two small cars are needed to carry 42 people.
● Any number of people between 40 and 50 can be carried without any
car having empty seats.

Review
● Review the correct solution, drawing out the strategies employed. If a
grid layout (see left) has not featured in the discussion, present this in
the form of a demonstration.
● Explain that, by listing each possible multiple of each vehicle type, all
possible combinations can be tested. Begin by connecting the 5 on the
list with each of the multiples of 8. Then repeat the process with the
10, stopping when a link to 32 gives the required combination.

Next steps
● Modify the capacity of each vehicle to give similar challenges. If the
numbers are reduced to 3 and 5, for example, it is possible to make any
number once the threshold value of 7 is exceeded.

Name _____

Big car, little car

■ Using both cars, how many of each car is needed to carry exactly 42 people? Each car must be full.

■ What other numbers of people between 40 and 50 can be carried without any cars having empty seats?

Target numbers

Learning objectives
(Y3) Knowledge strand: Derive and recall multiplication facts for the 2, 3, 4, 5, 6 and 10 times-tables and the corresponding division facts.
(Y3) Knowledge strand: Use knowledge of number operations and corresponding inverses to check calculations.
(Y4) Use/apply strand: Identify and use patterns, relationships and properties of numbers or shapes; investigate a statement involving numbers and test it with examples.

Expected prior knowledge
● Use the four operations, sometimes in combination, reliably.

You will need
Photocopiable page 41 (one per child).

Key vocabulary
number sentence, brackets, operation, approximately, adjust, addition, subtraction, multiplication, division

Brainteaser links
5: 'Number hunt' on page 12.
8: 'Just 19' on page 13.

Activity introduction
● Write the digits 8, 4, 2 and 1 and the symbols ×, + and − on a whiteboard.
● Invite the children to make 20, using two or more of the digits (and one or more of the operations) in combination. Each digit may be used only once but the symbols can be re-used. See what other numbers can be made between 20 and 30 (listed right are some example solutions).
● Discourage the temptation simply to put the digits together (such as 2 and 1 to create 21).
● Ask questions: *What would get you near to the target number? What other operation might we use here? Is this target number possible?*

$$20 = 8 × 2 + 4$$
$$21 = 8 × 2 + 4 + 1$$
$$22 = (8 + 1) × 2 + 4$$
$$23 = (8 + 4) × 2 - 1$$
$$24 = 8 × (2 + 1)$$
$$25 = (8 + 4) × 2 + 1$$
$$26 = (8 + 4 + 1) × 2$$
$$27 \text{ is not possible}$$
$$28 = (2 + 1) × 8 + 4$$
$$29 = 8 × 4 - 2 - 1$$
$$30 = 8 × 4 - 2$$

● Sometimes brackets are necessary for mathematical correctness. If this is a new idea you may need to consider how strictly this will be enforced in the next section.

Activity development
● Provide each child with a copy of photocopiable page 41. Explain that this activity extends the task to include all four operations.
● Begin with the worked example and use the term 'number sentence' to describe the given answer.
● Sometimes it will be possible to arrive at a correct solution in more than one way.
● If necessary, enlarge the sheet and use it as a shared task. This should allow both a quicker rate of completion and opportunities to correct mistakes.
● Where brackets are required but omitted, you should ask the child to explain their working before any amendment.

Review
● Sample some of the target numbers and identify whether it was possible, at certain points, to create a run of solutions where just minor changes to the number sentence were necessary.
● Identify places where the operation of division was (or could be) employed.
● Review the use of brackets and clarify the point that, in the absence of brackets, multiplication and division take precedence over addition and subtraction. Some children may still have a tendency to think that the order of presentation within a sentence governs the priority.

Next steps
● Consider opportunities to undertake similar tasks with the higher single-digit numbers, using target numbers above 50. This will be practicable only if children are confident with handling the higher multiples involved.

Target numbers

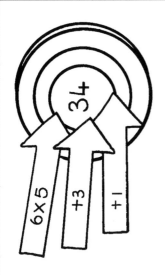

- Try to make these numbers from the digits 1, 2, 3, 4, 5 and 6 only.
- You can add, subtract, multiply or divide.
- Each time you may use each digit only once (although the symbols can be re-used). One has already been done for you as an example.

25	26	27	28	29
30	31	32	33	34
35	36	37	38	39 $6 \times 5 + 3 + 1$
40	41	42	43	44
45	46	47	48	49

Multiple puzzle

Learning objectives
(Y4) Use/apply strand:
Identify and use patterns, relationships and properties of numbers or shapes; investigate a statement involving numbers and test it with examples.
(Y4) Knowledge strand:
Derive and recall multiplication facts up to 10 × 10, the corresponding division facts and multiples of numbers to 10 up to the tenth multiple.

Expected prior knowledge
● Work with multiples.

You will need
Large sorting rings and cards/labels (or use an interactive whiteboard if available); photocopiable page 43 (one per child); scissors (one pair per child).

Key vocabulary
multiple, divisible, multiplication fact, number sentence, solution

Brainteaser link
5: 'Number hunt' on page 12.

Activity introduction
● Present two sorting rings, overlapping to give an intersection set (see right). Label each ring as shown and offer a selection of numbers for sorting.
● If the children are unfamiliar with the idea of an intersection set, the rings can be presented initially as discrete sets. When a given number can occupy both sets, the physical sliding of the two rings will offer a solution to this problem.
● Question the children to see if they have a good recall of multiples and/or can quickly derive answers from known facts. Lead the children towards the idea that numbers within the intersection represent the multiples of 6.
● Ask questions: *How did you work it out? Where will this number sit? Are all multiples of 3 odd?*
● If appropriate, you may want to introduce/revise the divisibility rule for 3 – that is, the sum of the digits will total 3 or a multiple thereof.

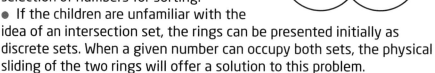
multiple of 2   multiple of 3

Activity development
● Give each child a copy of photocopiable page 43 and a pair of scissors. The task itself is self-explanatory but you may need to encourage them to use trial and improvement when they find that their first attempt at a solution is not going to work.
● Use this activity as an opportunity to observe and, as necessary, review divisibility rules. For example: a multiple of 2 is an even number; a multiple of 5 ends in 0 or 5; a multiple of 4 can be halved twice and the answer will still be a whole number.
● If the task proves unduly difficult, consider losing a panel (for example, a multiple of 6) and correspondingly reduce the range of the number cards to 1-8.

Solution
● One possible solution is: ×6 42; ×5 35; ×4 16; ×3 87; ×2 90.

Review
● Return to the sorting ring and change the labels to look at other multiples. When finished, look at the intersection set to see if any general rule can be provided for these numbers (for example, the intersection of multiples of 3 and multiples of 4 is the set of multiples of 12; use such an observation to add another number directly into that region).
● Review the main activity to see if there was a preferable order of attack. It is often considered best to tackle the more constrained multiples first, leaving the generous ones for when the number of available number cards is limited.

Next steps
● The complexity of the multiples can be increased by replacing the panel labelled 'Multiple of 2' with 'Multiple of 7'.

Multiple puzzle

■ Cut out the 0–9 number cards.
■ Put them in the ten squares below so that each two-digit answer is correct.
■ Is there more than one solution for each?

Multiple of 6

Multiple of 5

Multiple of 4

Multiple of 3

Multiple of 2

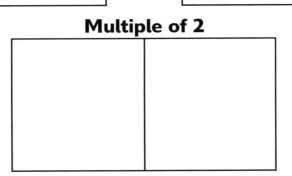

0	1	2	3	4
5	6	7	8	9

Multiple dominoes

Learning objectives
(Y3) Knowledge strand:
Derive and recall multiplication facts for the 2, 3, 4, 5, 6 and 10 times-tables and the corresponding division facts.
(Y4) Use/apply strand:
Represent a problem using number sentences, statements or diagrams; use these to solve the problem; present and interpret the solution in the context of the problem.

Expected prior knowledge
● Recall or derive quickly multiplication facts.
● Use the division symbol.
● Understand division as the inverse of multiplication.

You will need
Large multiplication grid or 100-square; prepared set of dominoes using photocopiable page 45 copied onto card or paper (use paper if you want children to stick the dominoes to a page as a permanent record of their work), enlarged in size if wished (one per group of up to three children).

Key vocabulary
same value, times-tables facts, number sentence, product, multiplied by, answer, factors, multiples

Brainteaser link
5: 'Number hunt' on page 12.

Activity introduction
● Ask some direct rapid-fire questions involving table facts previously introduced.
● Ask questions which demonstrate the inverse operation of division, such as: *How many groups of five can we make if we have 20 objects?*
● Use a large number square or completed multiplication grid to establish numbers which feature several times in times-table facts. Use this to develop the idea of factors and multiples.

Activity development
● Although it may appear that the puzzle has one unique solution, it has been designed to work in lots of different combinations. One example is shown below. In most cases a satisfactory arrangement will simply fall out by itself, with the two statements at each end being equivalent in value. At worst you will be left with one or more dominoes outside the loop. In such cases, it should always be possible to incorporate these pieces by breaking the loop at appropriate points.
● Observe how the children interact, the language they use, how they overcome difficulties and what calculation strategies they use (for number facts which are not known).
● Ask questions: *How do you know/derive that answer? How else can that number be made using multiplication? What other factors does this number have?*

Solution

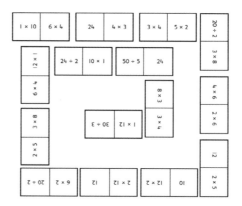

Review
● Choose some of the statements featured on the dominoes and ask selected children to create a word problem using the language of multiplication and/or division.
● Create a word bank for multiplication/division.

Next steps
● Develop recall of other table facts by creating a matching game using (say) ten pairs of cards. A number sentence must be matched to its answer (for example, 3 × 8 matches to 24). Alternatively you could create a set where a number sentence is matched by another number sentence of equivalent value (for example, 2 × 6 and 3 × 4). Arrange the cards face down as an array and play as in the game of 'pairs' (pelmanism).

Multiple dominoes

◤ Join each domino with another so that both halves have the same value.

◤ This puzzle can be completed in lots of different ways. See if you can use every domino!

1 × 10	6 × 4	50 ÷ 5	24	10	12 × 2
2 × 12	12	6 × 4	12 × 1	24	4 × 3
3 × 4	5 × 2	1 × 12	30 ÷ 3	4 × 6	2 × 6
24 ÷ 2	10 × 1	12	2 × 5	20 ÷ 2	3 × 8
6 × 2	20 ÷ 2	8 × 3	3 × 4	2 × 5	3 × 8

Three of a kind

Learning objectives
(Y3) Knowledge strand:
Derive and recall multiplication facts for the 3 times-table and the corresponding division facts.
(Y4) Use/apply strand:
Identify and use patterns, relationships and properties of numbers or shapes; investigate a statement involving numbers and test it with examples.

Expected prior knowledge
● Recall or calculate common multiples of 3 to 30 and identify other two-digit multiples beyond this (63, for example).

You will need
Counting stick or number line; photocopiable page 47 (one per pair); set of 0-9 number cards (one per pair).

Key vocabulary
multiple of 3, how many, times, multiply, multiplied by

Brainteaser link
5: 'Number hunt' on page 12.

Activity introduction
● Use a counting stick or number line with 'stations' to record the multiples of 3 from 0 to 30 (zero is a multiple of 3). Try to mark these points in a way other than simply counting on from zero (for example, by illustrating 15 as the midpoint between 0 and 30).
● Revise counting in 3s from 30 back down to 0. Consider using a number line to show the jumps from one multiple to the next.
● Count on in steps of 30 from 0 to 90. Explain that these steps are also multiples of 3. Represent these points on a 0-100 number line.
● Present some two-digit numbers beyond 30 and discuss ways in which such multiples can be 'projected' (for example, by counting on or back from 30, 60 or 90). Return to the number line, showing children how to find multiples of 3 in the vicinity of multiples of 30.
● Do not discuss the conventional divisibility rule for the 3 times-table, as this is saved for the Review session.

Activity development
● Provide each pair of children with a copy of photocopiable page 47 and a set of 0-9 number cards. Explain that the two cells allow either a single-digit entry (such as 6) or a double-digit entry (such as 27). If a single-digit number is played, the left-hand cell is simply left unoccupied.
● Remind the children to consider numbers beyond 30, particularly if the lower number cards have already been used.
● Ask questions: *Is that a multiple of 3? How do you know? What multiples do you know that are near to this number?*
● Observe the children taking turns, watching to ensure that answers given are actual multiples of 3.
● Observe which children appear to be more daring in their choice of (larger) numbers.

Review
● Talk to the group about the outcomes of the activity. It may have surprised them to find that all the number cards can (and should) be used in each game. This relates to the fact that the sum of the numbers 0 to 9 is 45.
● Discuss the divisibility rule for multiples of 3 (that is, the sum of the digits will always be a multiple of 3).

Next steps
● Extend the game by using two sets of 0-9 number cards and by increasing the number of cells to three (to allow up to three-digit numbers).

Name _____

Three of a kind

◼ Using a set of 0–9 number cards, take turns to place a one-digit or two-digit multiple of 3 in the boxes below.

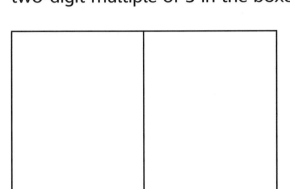
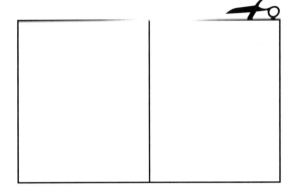
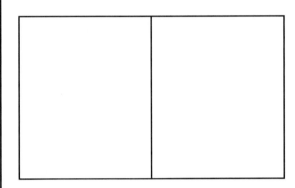
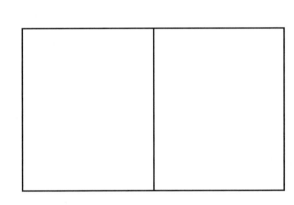
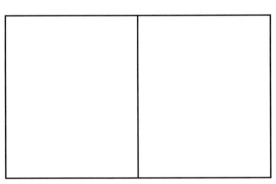
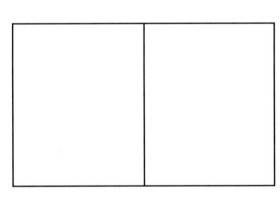
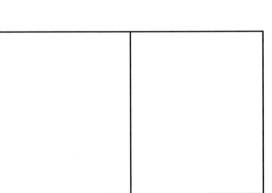
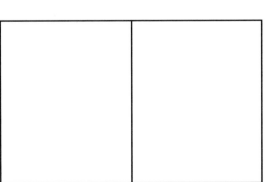

Hit the target

Activity introduction

● Hold a counting stick (or a 0-10 number line with the numerals removed) and practise counting in steps of 2 from 0 to 20, and back. Next, pick random multiples by pointing at a mark on the scale and asking the group for the appropriate answer. Use this to talk about strategies, such as knowing that 'halfway' is 10 and using this to count on/back to near multiples.

● Repeat the above for multiples such 5, 10 and 20. This will develop some of the skills needed later in the lesson.

● Ask questions: *How did you get that answer? Is there a different way?*

Activity development

● Hand out copies of photocopiable page 49 and refer to the numbers available.

● Talk about the strategies involved in 'hitting' the target numbers, such as using a multiple of 10 in combination with one or more single digits to get an approximation to the target number.

● Brackets are required when an operation needs to be carried out in an order different from the usual rules of precedence, and they add a layer of complexity to the activity. You may want to relax your expectations over the use of brackets if you are satisfied that an oral explanation of results is numerically accurate.

● Compare solutions to show how the same answer can often be achieved in different ways.

● Ask questions: *What will you try first? Can you get a closer approximation to that number?*

● If time allows, try the extension task at the foot of photocopiable page 49. To add variety, target numbers can be exchanged as mini challenges between group members.

Review

● Ask the children to mentally calculate the number sentence $6 \times (2 + 3) = 30$. Draw attention to the brackets showing that the addition must be carried out first.

● Next, provide children with simple (non-scientific) calculators and ask them to key in the number sentence and find the answer.

● In the absence of brackets, a non-scientific calculator will give an answer of 15 as it will tackle the calculations in the order they are entered. The key point which arises is that brackets are often needed in recording two-step calculations.

Learning objectives
(Y4) Use/apply strand:
Solve one-step and two-step problems involving numbers, money or measures, including time; choose and carry out appropriate calculations.
(Y4) Knowledge strand:
Derive and recall multiplication facts up to 10×10, the corresponding division facts and multiples of numbers to 10 up to the tenth multiple.

Expected prior knowledge
● Multiply single-digit numbers by multiples of 10.
● Carry out calculations involving more than one step.

You will need
Counting stick; photocopiable page 49 (one per child); simple (non-scientific) calculators (one per child).

Key vocabulary
multiplied by, approximate, nearest multiple, product, add, subtract, difference, method

Brainteaser links
5: 'Number hunt' on page 12.
14: 'Numbers up' on page 15.

Next steps
● Change the scale of the target numbers and/or explore calculation using other multiples of 10.
● Develop activities which require children to apply their use of multi-step calculations in contexts such as money. Using a target amount of £2.56, for example, the challenge could be to decide how many coins of denomination no greater than 20p would be needed to reach that figure.

Hit the target

◼ Use some or all of these numbers in calculations to hit the target numbers below.

20	10	6
2	3	4

◼ Make some other three-digit target numbers of your own.

Fraction dominoes

Learning objectives
(Y4) Use/apply strand:
Represent a problem using number sentences, statements or diagrams; use these to solve the problem; present and interpret the solution in the context of the problem.
(Y4) Knowledge strand:
Identify pairs of fractions that total 1.

Expected prior knowledge
● Work with non-unit fractions and fractions with a range of denominators.
● Calculate a fraction of a whole and a fraction of a quantity.

You will need
Fraction wall (see activity introduction); prepared set of dominoes using photocopiable page 51 copied onto card or paper (use paper if you want children to stick the dominoes to a page as a permanent record of their work), enlarged in size if wished (one per pair/group).

Key vocabulary
same value, fraction, numerator, denominator, factor

Brainteaser link
5: 'Number hunt' on page 12.

Activity introduction

● Look at the fraction wall below. Talk about the equivalent fractions that can be deduced by visual reference to the wall.
● Show how a 'fraction family' for any given unit fraction (one half, for example) can be generated by multiplying the numerator and denominator by 2, 3, 4 and so on.

1											
$\frac{1}{2}$						$\frac{1}{2}$					
$\frac{1}{4}$		$\frac{1}{4}$		$\frac{1}{4}$			$\frac{1}{4}$				
$\frac{1}{8}$	$\frac{1}{8}$	$\frac{1}{8}$	$\frac{1}{8}$	$\frac{1}{8}$	$\frac{1}{8}$	$\frac{1}{8}$	$\frac{1}{8}$				
$\frac{1}{12}$	$\frac{1}{12}$	$\frac{1}{12}$	$\frac{1}{12}$	$\frac{1}{12}$	$\frac{1}{12}$	$\frac{1}{12}$	$\frac{1}{12}$	$\frac{1}{12}$	$\frac{1}{12}$	$\frac{1}{12}$	$\frac{1}{12}$

Activity development

● Provide each pair or group with a set of dominoes from photocopiable page 51. The task requires each domino half to be joined to another domino to give a total of one whole unit (for example, $^3/_4$ and $^2/_8$).
● The puzzle has been designed to work in lots of different combinations (one example is shown below). In most cases a satisfactory arrangement will simply fall out by itself, with the two statements at each end combining to total one whole unit. At worst, you will be left with one or more dominoes outside the loop. In such cases, it should always be possible to incorporate these pieces by breaking the loop at appropriate points.
● Ask questions: *How do you know that these fractions share the same value? How can that fraction be simplified? What factor do both digits in the fraction share?*

Solution

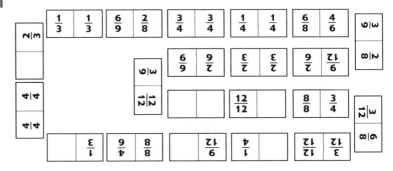

Review

● Ask selected children to create a word problem using the language of fractions (for example, within a money context).
● To meet the learning objectives fully, identify other pairs of fractions which give a total of 1.

Next steps
● Develop recall of other fractions by creating a matching game using, for example, ten pairs of cards. A fraction must be matched to another of equivalent value. Arrange the cards face down as an array and play as in the game of 'pairs' (pelmanism).

Fraction dominoes

		$\frac{3}{9}$	$\frac{2}{8}$	$\frac{3}{9}$	$\frac{12}{12}$
	$\frac{1}{4}$	$\frac{6}{9}$	$\frac{2}{8}$	$\frac{2}{3}$	$\frac{2}{3}$
$\frac{1}{3}$		$\frac{3}{12}$	$\frac{6}{8}$	$\frac{6}{8}$	$\frac{4}{6}$
	$\frac{2}{3}$	$\frac{3}{12}$	$\frac{12}{12}$	$\frac{8}{8}$	$\frac{4}{6}$
$\frac{9}{12}$		$\frac{1}{3}$	$\frac{1}{3}$	$\frac{3}{4}$	$\frac{3}{4}$
$\frac{12}{12}$		$\frac{2}{6}$	$\frac{6}{9}$	$\frac{8}{8}$	$\frac{3}{4}$
$\frac{1}{4}$	$\frac{1}{4}$	$\frac{9}{12}$	$\frac{2}{6}$	$\frac{4}{4}$	$\frac{4}{4}$

Snack bar

Learning objectives
(Y4) Knowledge strand:
Use knowledge of addition and subtraction facts and place value to derive sums and differences of pairs of multiples of 10.
(Y5) Use/apply strand:
Solve one-step and two-step problems involving whole numbers and decimals and all four operations, choosing and using appropriate methods, including calculator use.

Expected prior knowledge
● Carry out calculations involving £.p notation.

You will need
Photocopiable page 53 (one per child); money and/or calculators (both optional).

Key vocabulary
combinations, difference, altogether, total, change, how many?

Brainteaser links
2: 'Hidden answers' on page 11.
15: 'Chocolate selection' on page 16.

Activity introduction
● Present an enlarged version of photocopiable page 53. Explain the context of a snack bar from which shoppers can buy any combination of the items featured. Add some amounts underneath each item, at a level which you know the children are likely to manage (for example, all prices could be multiples of 5).
● Ask questions: *How many bars of chocolate could I buy with £1? What change (if any) would I receive (from the above)? How much would it cost me to have one of each item? If I bought three items and the total cost was ___ , what were the three items? What three items would you buy, and what would be their total?*
● Take every opportunity to discuss various strategies, such as building totals by starting from the highest priced item.

Activity development
● Provide each child with photocopiable page 53. Explain that this time, the cost of each item is unknown and the only clues lie in their combined totals.
● Begin by looking at the box featuring just the drink and the apple, inviting individual children to suggest what each item might cost.
● Let the children work individually or in pairs. Observe both the quality of communication and engagement with the mathematics.
● Ask questions: *How did you find the solution? Is there another way of working it out?*
● The task has been designed to enable access to the mathematics in several ways. Looking at the two combinations of paired items, for example, it can be seen that a drink with an apple costs 20p more than a packet of crisps with an apple, so a drink must cost 20p more than a packet of crisps. Similarly, the two triple combinations differ by 10p, so an apple must cost 10p more than a packet of crisps.
● Some children will benefit from a supply of coins and/or a calculator.
● If the core task proves too challenging, consider reducing the price of each item and/or reduce the number of items to three.

Solution
● Apple 40p; crisps 30p; drink 50p; chocolate 60p.

Review
● Explore different strategies for solving the problem. Give credit for all strategies, including those which proved quite inefficient.
● With an agreement on the solution, return to questions of the type sampled earlier (looking at the cost of multiples of any one item).

Next steps
● Create a harder task by establishing five differently priced items on a familiar theme. Produce a few combinations which offer sufficient information to deduce the price of each item.
● Make each price a value other than a multiple of 10p. This will not only make the task more arithmetically challenging, it will also encourage methods other than trial and improvement.

Snack bar

■ Calculate how much each individual item costs.

Give and take

Activity introduction

● Locate a multiple of 10 and a smaller near-multiple of 10 on a number line (for example, 70 and 48). Ask the children what we mean by the word 'difference' when it is used in a mathematical context. Emphasise that the difference between two numbers is always positive, unlike in a subtraction sentence where the order of the two numbers must be carefully considered.

● Calculate the difference between the two numbers by counting on from the smaller number, initially to the next multiple of 10. Label the size of each jump at each stage.

● Consider finding the difference between two non-multiples of 10, using the nearest multiples of 10 (above and below) as bridging points.

● Talk about other ways of calculating the difference, such as counting on in 10s from the smaller number.

● Try finding a difference using a counting back method (starting from the larger number).

Activity development

● Provide each child or pair with a set of 1–9 number cards and photocopiable page 55. Provide a supply of equipment appropriate to the group's needs (see 'You will need').

● Begin with a relatively easy example, such as the difference between 21 and 12, the two numbers which can be created using 1 and 2.

● Set the children working on the task independently or in pairs, encouraging them to use any method of calculation.

● Look at how children make use of any equipment, if this is required (in some cases individuals may well be able to calculate the difference using mental approaches alone).

● Encourage the group to use the reverse of the photocopiable sheet (or individual whiteboards) to try further examples.

● Ask questions: *How did you find that difference? What will you do next? How might you check the answer?*

● Encourage the group to check their answers by adding the difference to the smaller number.

Review

● Gather some of the answers and ask the group what they notice about all the answers (they are all multiples of 9). The reason for this is quite complex and likely to be beyond all but the most exceptional child. Algebraically, the two numbers made from any two cards, a and b, would have values of $10a + b$ and $10b + a$. When the latter is subtracted from the former, the answer is $9a - 9b$, or $9(a - b)$. Any solution is therefore a multiple of 9.

● If any answers are not multiples of 9, work through some or all of these to identify the error. If such an error is common across the group, identify the nature of the problem.

Learning objectives
(Y3) Knowledge strand:
Use knowledge of number operations and corresponding inverses to check calculations.
(Y4) Use/apply strand:
Identify and use patterns, relationships and properties of numbers or shapes; investigate a statement involving numbers and test it with examples.

Expected prior knowledge
● Find differences between two-digit numbers, using any mental/written methods including jottings.

You will need
Demonstration 0–100 number line; 1–9 number cards (one set per child/pair); photocopiable page 55 (one per child); number lines/bead strings/paper to aid calculation (as required); individual whiteboards (optional).

Key vocabulary
how many more, pattern, multiple, difference, smaller, larger, subtraction

Brainteaser link
4: 'Puzzle corner' on page 12.

Next steps
● Consider repeating the activity with three-digit numbers and, once again, review the answers derived.

Give and take

- Choose two cards from a set of 1–9 number cards.
- Make the largest number you can with them.
- Now make the smallest number.
- What is the difference between the two numbers?
- Repeat the activity for more pairs of numbers.

largest	smallest	difference

largest	smallest	difference

largest	smallest	difference

largest	smallest	difference

largest	smallest	difference

- Look at your answers. What do you notice? _____

_____

Perfect numbers

Learning objectives
(Y4) Use/apply strand:
Identify and use patterns, relationships and properties of numbers or shapes; investigate a statement involving numbers and test it with examples.
(Y5) Knowledge strand:
Identify pairs of factors of two-digit whole numbers and find common multiples (for example, for 6 and 9).

Expected prior knowledge
● Recall or find mentally multiples of numbers.
● Explain the concept of division with reference to sharing.

You will need
24 large counters/cubes; photocopiable page 57 (one per child); counters/squared paper (optional).

Key vocabulary
half, odd, even

Brainteaser link
4: 'Number hunt' on page 12.

Activity introduction
● Present 24 large counters/cubes and invite individuals to create a rectangular array (for example, 8 by 3). Relate these outcomes to the multiplication facts they represent, recording them as number sentences (for example, $8 \times 3 = 24$).
● For each array, develop statements that use the vocabulary (for example '3 and 8 are factors of 24'; '24 is a multiple of 3'; '24 is a multiple of 8').
● Encourage the children to find all the factors of a number, not forgetting 1 and the number itself.
● If time allows, explore other numbers. Check that the children are developing a sense of the type of numbers which have many factors (for example, multiples of 12).

Activity development
● Provide each child with photocopiable page 57 and, if considered appropriate, either counters or squared paper to create arrays featuring their chosen numbers.
● Use this activity as an opportunity to apply divisibility rules (for example, numbers with a digit root of 3, or a multiple thereof, will be divisible by 3).
● If children need to use visual methods, restrict the numbers to make sure this is practical (for example, use only numbers to 24).

Review
● The title of the activity has a specific significance in that there is a set of numbers thought to be 'perfect'. The sum of the factors of a perfect number, excluding the number itself, is equal to the number.
● The example featured on the photocopiable sheet is therefore perfect as the sum of 1, 2 and 3 gives 6.
● Invite children to find the only other perfect number below 30 (see solution below).

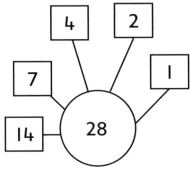

A perfect number: $1 + 2 + 4 + 7 + 14 = 28$

Next steps
● When reviewing the work covered, it is likely that most of the numbers explored will have an even number of factors. The exceptions will be square numbers.
● Encourage children to review a range of square numbers, inviting them to reason why this is the case (the square root of such a number is 'multiplied by itself').

Perfect numbers

6 is a multiple of 1, 2, 3 and 6.
These numbers are called its factors.

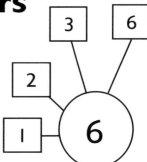

◼ Find the factors of some other numbers.
◼ What other numbers have lots of factors?

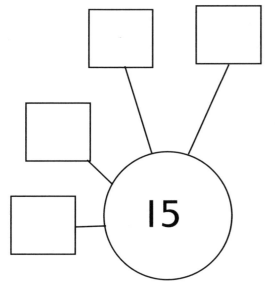

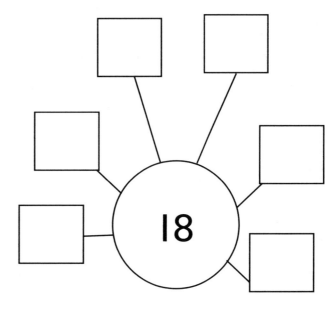

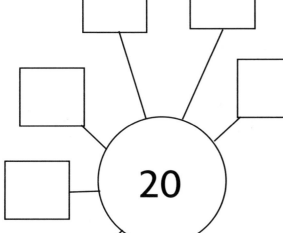

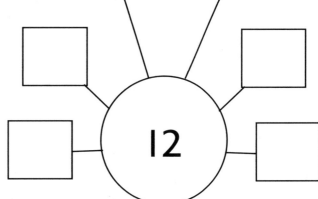

Number triplets

Learning objectives
(Y3) Calculate strand: Add or subtract mentally combinations of one-digit and two-digit numbers.
(Y4) Use/apply strand: Identify and use patterns, relationships and properties of numbers or shapes; investigate a statement involving numbers and test it with examples.

Expected prior knowledge
● Recall rapidly number bonds up to a total of 20.
● Add three given numbers reliably.

You will need
Individual whiteboards; photocopiable page 59 (one per child); scissors (one pair per child).

Key vocabulary
total, equal, segment, odd, even, combination

Brainteaser link
7: 'That's odd' on page 13.

Activity introduction
● Provide individual whiteboards and ask for any three different numbers with a total of 10. Compare and contrast different solutions. Ask: *Are there any other ways?*
● Choose other target totals in the range 11 to 20 and repeat in the same way.

Activity development
● Provide each child with photocopiable page 59 and a pair of scissors. Explain the task as presented.
● Observe the children arranging the tiles across the diagram, noting the strategy employed by individuals. Some may work randomly initially, with some trial and improvement as they try to establish a balance of numbers. Others may be more deliberate in reasoning, for example placing 1, 2 and 3 in separate segments and then adding a second layer using 4, 5 and 6. With this approach, the final three numbers will either fall into place successfully or, if not, the second layer will need amendment.
● Note that there are two distinctly different solutions (see below): children finishing early could be asked to find the alternative arrangement as an extension.
● Ask questions: *What strategy did you use to find a solution? Is there another way? What is the total of each segment and why is it this amount?*

Solutions
1, 5, 9	1, 6, 8
2, 6, 7	2, 4, 9
3, 4, 8	3, 5, 7

Review
● Discuss the solutions, including the way that even and odd numbers are distributed within each segment. The segment total (15) is odd and can be made only from 'odd, odd, odd' or 'even, even, odd'. Furthermore, the fact that the range of numbers features more odd than even numbers 'forces' certain combinations.
● If the total of the entire range of numbers has not yet been mentioned, it is worth demonstrating that the sum of each segment (15) can be deduced from the fact that the total of all three segments is 45 (the sum of the numbers 1 to 9).
● When considering whether all possibilities have been found, one approach is to establish that 1 must feature somewhere. In order to achieve a segment total of 15, the two other numbers in that segment must add up to 14, which can be done in only two ways: 5 and 9 or 6 and 8.

Next steps
● The activity can be made more challenging by using numbers other than the multiples of 1; for example, the multiples of 2 from 2 to 18.

Number triplets

■ Cut out the numbers 1–9 at the foot of the page and arrange them in the spaces so that each of the three major segments has the same total.

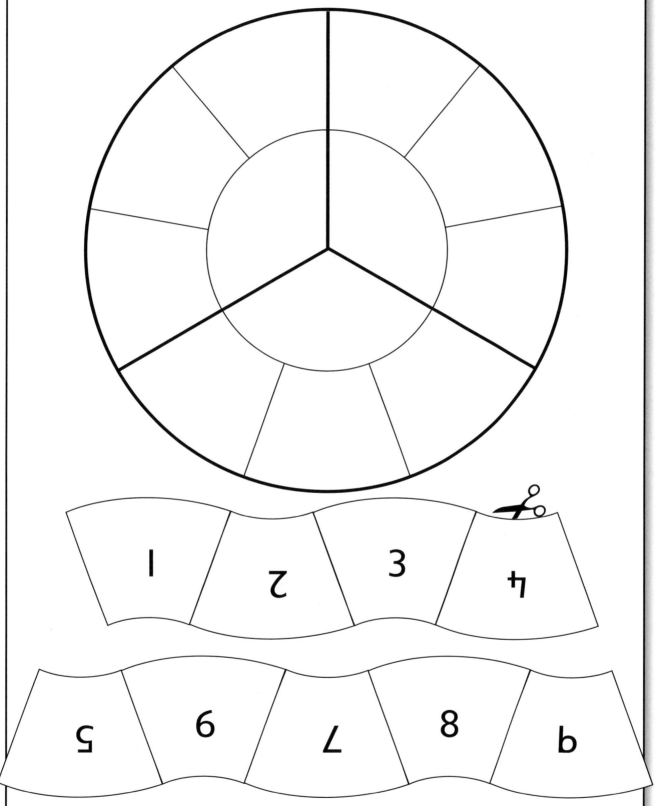

20 up

Learning objectives
(Y3) Calculate strand: Add or subtract mentally combinations of one-digit and two-digit numbers.
(Y4) Use/apply strand: Identify and use patterns, relationships and properties of numbers or shapes; investigate a statement involving numbers and test it with examples.

Expected prior knowledge
● Recall and use number bonds up to and including 20.
● Recognise that addition can be done in any order.
● Add any given three numbers reliably.

You will need
Individual whiteboards; photocopiable page 61 (one per child/pair); scissors.

Key vocabulary
combination, total, altogether, number sentence

Brainteaser link
8: 'Just 19' on page 13.

Activity introduction
● Provide individual whiteboards and ask for any three different numbers with a total of 20. Compare and contrast different solutions. Ask: *Are there any other ways?*
● Use this as an opportunity to identify useful strategies such as: using known near doubles before adding a third number; finding a convenient pairing to 10; adding two small numbers and making the total up to 20.
● If time allows, repeat the activity using a different target number in the range 11 to 30. You could also vary the number of numbers added to make the target number.

Activity development
● Provide each child or pair of children with photocopiable page 61 along with a pair of scissors. Explain that the challenge is much like in the introduction activity, except that once a number card has been used as part of a set of three, it cannot be used in further sets.
● Encourage the children to arrange their cards in a linear and ordered fashion, as this helps with notions of pattern, compensation and so on.
● Explain that they may get stuck as early as the second or third set of cards as combinations become increasingly restricted.
● Encourage pairs of children to take turns in selecting sets of cards and not to intervene while their partner is calculating/selecting.
● When no further sets can be created, ask for the sets to be recorded before starting again.
● As implied by the instruction on photocopiable page 61, it is possible to create four sets of three cards within the range provided (see below). Make this clear if it appears that such a challenge would be motivating.

Solution
● The following four sets of numbers make a total of 20:
  1, 6, 13
  2, 8, 10
  3, 5, 12
  4, 7, 9

Review
● Review how successful individuals/pairs have been in creating sets of addition facts. Invite them to report back on their sets, identifying how many cards were used in total before getting stuck.
● If no one has reached a four-set solution, demonstrate the example given above. Note that this set uses every number in the first half of the range (that is, 1 to 10 inclusive).

Next steps
Provide related challenges using the same set of cards:
● Find four even numbers (all greater than 0) with a total of 20. (There is only one solution: 2, 4, 6, 8.)
● Find four odd numbers (all greater than 0) with a total of 20. (There are two solutions: 1, 3, 7, 9 and 1, 3, 5, 11.)

20 up

- Choose any three number cards with a total of 20.
- Now take another three cards with the same total.
- Can you take another set of three cards? And another?

1	**2**	**3**	**4**
5	**6**	**7**	**8**
9	**10**	**11**	**12**
13	**14**	**15**	**16**
17	**18**	**18**	**20**

Connections

Learning objectives
(Y3) Calculate strand: Add or subtract mentally combinations of one-digit and two-digit numbers.
(Y4) Use/apply strand: Report solutions to problems, giving explanations and reasoning orally and in writing.

Expected prior knowledge
● Recall rapidly addition and subtraction facts.

You will need
Photocopiable page 63 (one per child); scissors (one pair per child).

Key vocabulary
difference, total, equal, pattern

Brainteaser link
8: 'Just 19' on page 13.

Activity introduction
● Present an enlarged version of the spider diagram from photocopiable page 63 and lead a task based on the concept of difference. The task is to arrange the numbers 1 to 7 so that, for every straight line of three numbers, the central number (common to all) represents the difference between the opposing pairs (an example is shown here).
● Invite individual children to have a go and use this as an opportunity to discuss strategies.
● The correct solutions have 1, 2 or 4 at the centre. If the children find a solution simply through perseverance, they should be given due credit.
● The next stage is to tackle the challenge detailed on the photocopiable sheet, still working with the enlarged spider diagram as a group task. Explain that the task is not unlike the one just completed, but involves addition rather than subtraction. Begin by placing 4 at the centre and telling the group that, when completed, every straight line of three numbers must have the same total (see right for a possible solution).
● Ask questions: *Where would you start? Are there any patterns? Is the middle number important when we are looking for suitable pairings?*
● One possible strategy is to pair the six remaining numbers, perhaps starting with the smallest and largest numbers (1 and 7). The two remaining pairings must also share the same total of 8.

Activity development
● Provide each child with photocopiable page 63 and a pair of scissors. The task is to repeat the activity above, finding other solutions.
● The central number can only be 1, 4 or 7. The strategy of 'balancing' the three pairs of remaining numbers works equally well for 1 and 7 as it did for 4.
● Observe the children arranging the cards, noting the strategies employed. Some children may work randomly initially, with some trial and improvement as they try to equalise the totals. Others may be more deliberate in their reasoning, using the strategy outlined earlier.

Review
● Discuss the solutions, consolidating the fact that the problem works only when the central number is at the beginning, middle or end of the range.

Next steps
● A follow-up task can be created by replacing the numbers used with any consecutive sequence with a regular pattern. The numerical complexity of the task will increase, but it will still be true that the middle number must be at the beginning, middle or end of the range. Suggested number patterns include 5, 6, 7, 8, 9, 10, 11 and 10, 13, 16, 19, 22, 25, 28.

Connections

■ Cut out and arrange the 1–7 number cards so that every connected line of three numbers has the same total.

■ Are there other ways to arrange these numbers?

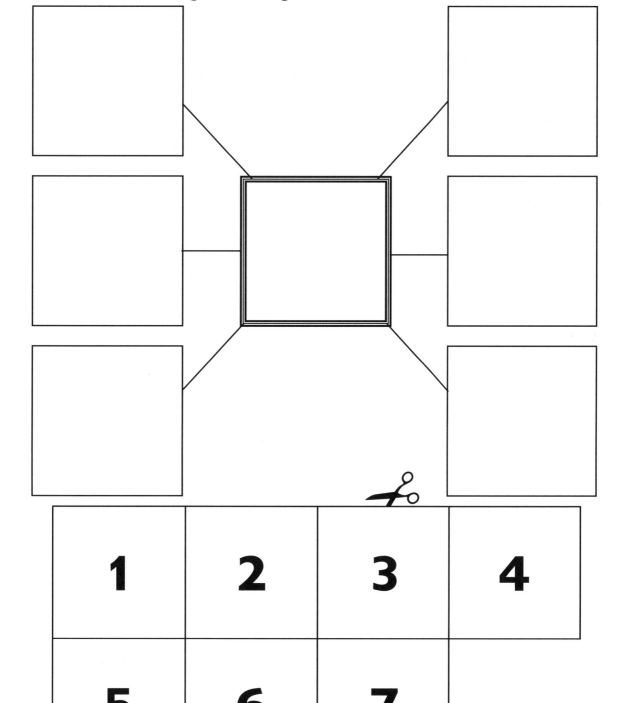

1	2	3	4
5	6	7	

Magic triangles

Learning objectives
(Y3) Calculate strand: Add or subtract mentally combinations of one-digit and two-digit numbers.
(Y4) Use/apply strand: Report solutions to problems, giving explanations and reasoning orally and in writing.

Expected prior knowledge
● Recall rapidly subtraction facts (difference).

You will need
Enlarged and modified version of photocopiable page 65 (see activity introduction); photocopiable page 65 (one per child); scissors (one pair per child).

Key vocabulary
difference, strategy, adjacent, arrange, odd, even

Brainteaser link
8: 'Just 19' on page 13.

Activity introduction
● Use an enlarged and modified version of photocopiable page 65 to find arrangements of the digits 1 to 6 so that the totals of the three numbers along each side of the triangle are the same.
● Invite individuals to take turns in placing number cards. As and when an error arises, a card can be shifted from one place to another.
● There are four significantly different solutions (see below). The four strategies that lead to these solutions involve careful consideration of the numbers at the corners, which may be the lowest numbers, the highest numbers, the even numbers or the odd numbers.
● For each of the solutions the side total is unique, ranging from 9 (when the lowest numbers feature at the corners) through to 12 (when the highest numbers feature at the corners).
● Look to see if solutions are derived by trial and improvement, or by a more systematic approach.

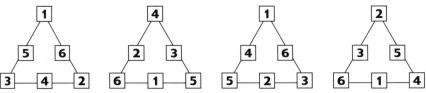

Activity development
● Provide each child with photocopiable page 65 and a pair of scissors. Explain the task as presented.
● Note the strategies the children use as they arrange the number cards across the diagram. Some may work randomly initially, with some trial and improvement as they try to establish correct separations. Others may be more deliberate in reasoning, recognising, for example, that a difference of 12 cannot be made, therefore 12 must be positioned at a corner. The two solutions are shown below.

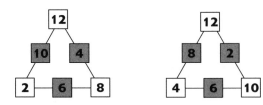

● Ask questions: *What strategy did you use to find a solution? Is there another way? What do you notice about the layout of the numbers?*
● The challenge can be made a little more accessible by reducing the sequence to the range 1 to 6.

Review
● Discuss the solutions, including the way that the corner numbers accompanying 12 have a mutual difference of 6 in both cases.

Next steps
● The photocopiable page can be made more challenging by using numbers other than multiples of 2. One such set might feature multiples of 7, from 7 to 42.

Name _____

Magic triangles

◢ Arrange one number in each space so that each shaded square shows the difference between the two corner numbers either side.

◢ Is there another way to arrange the numbers to achieve the same result?

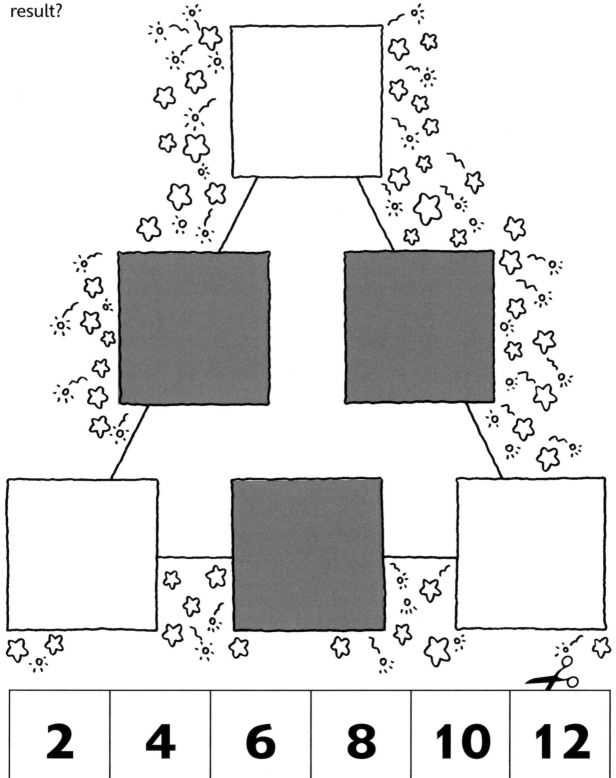

| 2 | 4 | 6 | 8 | 10 | 12 |

50 MATHS LESSONS · AGES 7-9

Crossovers

Activity introduction

● Arrange a set of 1–8 number cards in ascending order. Ask the children to calculate their total mentally. Gather answers and establish the actual total (36).
● Discuss different strategies, such as tackling each number in turn or choosing numbers which combine to give sub-totals of 10.
● Demonstrate how taking a card from each end of the range can give sub-totals of 9 (8 and 1, 7 and 2 and so on), establishing that the total is therefore 9 × 4.

Activity development

● Provide each child with photocopiable page 67 and a pair of scissors.
● Explain that this task requires addition of single digits in the range 1 to 8. The task should be fairly self-explanatory but you may need to clarify that the two central positions are part of both sets of numbers.
● Observe each child to see whether trial and improvement is used. You might ask questions to establish whether a more reasoned approach is being used. It will be encouraging for the children to know that there are several significantly different solutions.
● If some find it frustrating, the total for one of the solutions could be given. Alternatively, fixing two central numbers in position will make the task easier.

Solutions

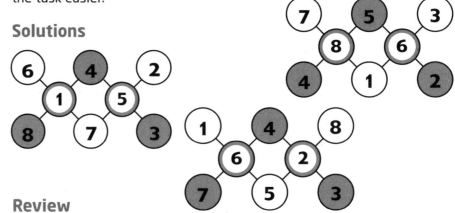

Review

● Gather together all the successful solutions found and encourage the children to look for similarities and differences. Pay particular attention to the central numbers.
● It may be useful to establish that the central numbers must be either both odd or both even (and as these two numbers are used in both sets of numbers, the overall total of the two sets will be the sum of the numbers 1 to 8 [36] plus these two numbers; the total of each set will be half of this overall total).
● Talk about which strategy worked best. On this occasion, trial and improvement may have been quicker than looking for a rational distribution of the numbers according to their relative value.

Next steps

● Particularly able children could investigate sequences of numbers other than 1 to 8. Any multiple of this set would be suitable.

Learning objectives
(Y4) Use/apply strand: Identify and use patterns, relationships and properties of numbers or shapes; investigate a statement involving numbers and test it with examples.
(Y4) Use/apply strand: Report solutions to problems, giving explanations and reasoning orally and in writing.

Expected prior knowledge
● Add several single digits reliably.
● Tackle number puzzles.

You will need
A set of 1–8 number cards; photocopiable page 67 (one per child); scissors (one pair per child).

Key vocabulary
total, addition, equal, compensate, difference, arrangement

Brainteaser link
10: 'Shape mix' on page 14.

Name _____

Crossovers

Cut out and position the 1–8 number cards so that the numbers in the grey circles have the same total as the numbers in the white circles. Notice that two of the circles are both grey and white – this is because they are part of both sets of numbers.

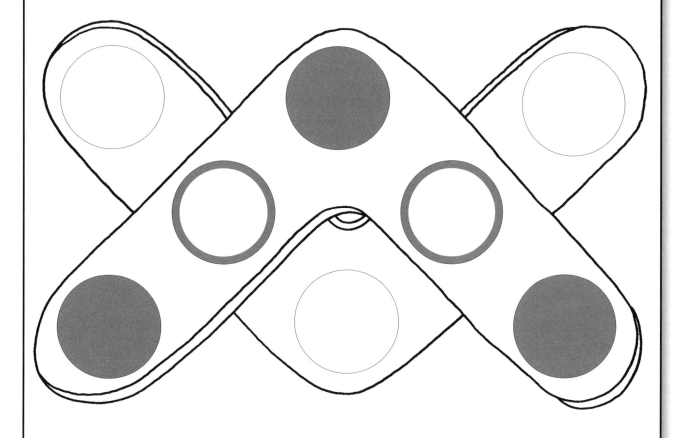

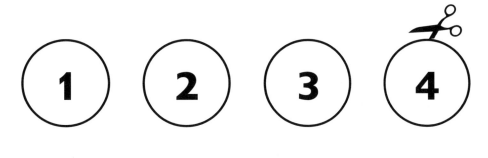

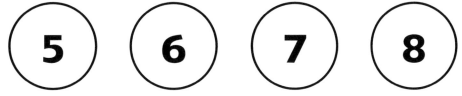

Intersections

Activity introduction

● Arrange a set of three counters to represent a right-angled triangle. Explain that 3 is known as a triangular number and show how the arrangement of counters demonstrates this fact. Now invite individuals to show you why 6 is the next triangular number (1 + 2 + 3).

● Extend the sequence and record the triangular numbers with the accompanying calculation (1 + 2 + 3 + 4 and so on).

Activity development

● Provide each child or pair of children with photocopiable page 69 and a set of suitably sized 1-12 number cards (a set can be taken from photocopiable page 61 if necessary).

● Explain that this task will require lots of addition of single digits to totals (possibly up to 50). The task should be fairly self-explanatory but you may need to clarify that two of the positions are part of both sets of numbers.

● Observe each child to see whether trial and improvement is used. You might ask questions to establish what strategies are being used.

● It will be encouraging to know that there are several significantly different solutions (one is shown below).

● If some children find it frustrating, 'fixing' some numbers in position will make the task easier.

Solution

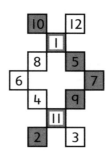

Review

● Gather together all the successful solutions found and encourage the children to look for similarities and differences. Pay particular attention to the two numbers which form the intersections.

● This is a complex puzzle to solve, even though there are several solutions.

● Talk about which strategy worked best. Trying to balance the numbers (by alternately placing those of a similar scale on the two tracks) seems to work well on most occasions. Often there is a small inequality between the two totals which can be eliminated by exchanging one number with another.

Next steps

● Triangular numbers could be researched further using internet search engines or a mathematical dictionary.

● Set a similar task looking at other types of number sequences (Fibonacci, square numbers and so on).

Learning objectives
(Y4) Use/apply strand:
Identify and use patterns, relationships and properties of numbers or shapes; investigate a statement involving numbers and test it with examples.
(Y4) Use/apply strand:
Report solutions to problems, giving explanations and reasoning orally and in writing.

Expected prior knowledge
● Add several single digits reliably.
● Tackle number puzzles.

You will need
Counters for demonstration; photocopiable page 69, enlarged if wished (one per child/pair); 1-12 number cards (one set per child/pair).

Key vocabulary
total, addition, equal, compensate, difference, arrangement, triangular number

Brainteaser link
8: 'Just 19' on page 13.

Intersections

◼ Use the digits 1 to 12 so that the numbers in the grey positions have the same total as the numbers in the white positions. Notice that two of the positions are both grey and white.

Stars and moons

Learning objectives
(Y3) Calculate strand: Add or subtract mentally combinations of one-digit numbers.
(Y4) Use/apply strand: Identify and use patterns, relationships and properties of numbers or shapes; investigate a statement involving numbers and test it with examples.

Expected prior knowledge
● Recall the multiples of 2, 3 and 4.

You will need
An enlarged version of each hat for demonstration; individual whiteboards; photocopiable page 71 (one per child/pair); multiple copies of each hat, cut out in card (optional).

Key vocabulary
combinations, total, altogether, multiple

Brainteaser links
8: 'Just 19' on page 13.
11: 'Target 34' on page 14.

Activity introduction
● Present an enlarged version of the hat which is represented on the right of photocopiable page 71. Ask questions: *If I had ten of this hat, how many stars/moons would I have? If I had 27 stars, how many hats would I have? Could I get exactly 50 stars?*
● Introduce the second hat and discuss the differences in design. Note how the hats have been presented differently by shading, to further distinguish their appearance.
● Ask related questions, this time providing individual whiteboards to support calculation: *If I had one of each hat, how many stars and how many moons would I have altogether? Can you calculate how many stars I would have if I chose five of each hat?*
● Discuss strategies for calculation, ensuring that the words 'combination' and 'total' are introduced.

Activity development
● Provide each child or pair of children with photocopiable page 71. Explain that this time, the required total number of stars and moons has been given. Children need to explore the possible combinations of different hat types to find those that achieve the total. Explain that the solution may be achieved by having more of one hat type than the other.
● Ask questions: *How did you find the solution? Is there another way of working it out?*
● Some children will benefit from a supply of card cut-outs of each hat, as this offers a more immediate visual model of the problem.
● Observe each child, noting the strategies used. Some children may adopt a trial and improvement approach by first selecting any reasonable combination of hats and then adjusting accordingly. Others may begin with multiples of one hat type and then replace or supplement with the other as the target is approached.

Review
● Begin this section by showing the successful combination of three dark hats and two light hats.
● Introduce the idea of lists (see right), where each row details successive multiples of each hat. Once the list is drawn up, it is easy to look across both blocks of information so that both conditions (stars and moons) are simultaneously satisfied (shown in bold).

	Dark hat		Light hat	
	Stars	Moons	Stars	Moons
×1	2	2	3	1
×2	4	4	**6**	**2**
×3	**6**	**6**	9	3
×4	8	8	12	4
×5	10	10	15	5
×6	12	12	18	6

Next steps
● Produce a related task where the total number of hats is given, along with the resultant number of stars and moons. This gives a more closed task for those needing further support/consolidation.
● Modify the ratio of hats and stars on one or both hats and repeat the task with a new target of stars and moons.

Name _____

Stars and moons

🔲 Pick a combination of these hat designs to give a total of 12 stars and 8 moons.

Money exchange

Learning objectives
(Y3) Calculate strand: Add or subtract mentally combinations of one-digit and two-digit numbers.
(Y4) Use/apply strand: Identify and use patterns, relationships and properties of numbers or shapes; investigate a statement involving numbers and test it with examples.

Expected prior knowledge
- Calculate quickly multiples of 2, 5 and 10.
- Add sub-totals reliably to 50.
- Use the featured coins.

You will need
Collections of featured coins (real or plastic); photocopiable page 73 (one per child).

Key vocabulary
coin, multiple, total, difference, amount

Brainteaser link
6: 'Cashing up' on page 13.

Activity introduction

- If using real coins, begin by discussing similarities and properties across the featured denominations. Talk about 'trivial' matters such as their visual appearance (colour, size, shape) before moving on to matters of equivalence.
- Ask questions: *How many of these coins would you exchange for one of these? Which is worth more, x of these or y of these? If I used x of these, how much change would I get from 50 pence?*

Activity development

- Without reference to photocopiable page 73, invite individual children to make 50p using any number of coins. Compare different solutions, noting the variations in the number of coins used.
- Provide copies of photocopiable page 73, paying particular attention to the grid of 16 cells. Explain that this has been included to make sure that exactly 16 coins are used. Read through the challenge with the class to check comprehension.
- Observe some of the early selections made by individuals. One possible strategy is to begin with two or three 10p coins and progressively reduce the denominations as the target amount is approached. Using this method, it is possible to get close to a solution which can be adjusted to suit.
- There is potential for a high level of success as there are several solutions (some of which are shown below).
- Ask questions: *How did you work that out? Have you checked your answer? Is there another way? How many more of these coins would you need?*

Solutions

1p	2p	5p	10p	Total
×5	×5	×5	×1	50p
×4	×8	×2	×2	50p
×8	×1	×6	×1	50p
×9	×3	×1	×3	50p

Review

- Use a table similar to that shown above to review successful combinations.
- Look for similarities in answers, particularly across examples where some of the multiples of specific denominations are common.
- The task lends itself well to the use of a prepared spreadsheet where each column is headed with the coin denomination. By restricting the total across any given combination to 16, it is possible to apply formulae to particular cells to enable experimentation.

Next steps
- Introduce the 20p coin and create similar problems where the total equals £1.00.

Money exchange

- Use 1p, 2p, 5p and 10p coins only.
- Put one coin in each space so that the total is exactly 50p.
- Are there other ways of making 50p?

© The Royal Mint

In the balance

Learning objectives
(Y3) Calculate strand: Add or subtract mentally combinations of one-digit and two-digit numbers.
(Y4) Use/apply strand: Represent a problem using number sentences and diagrams; use these to solve the problem; present and interpret the solution in the context of the problem.

Expected prior knowledge
● Use a real set of balance scales.

You will need
Demonstration set of number cards featuring 1, 2, 4, 8, 16, 32, 64; an enlarged version of photocopiable page 75 with a mass of 13 depicted on the left-hand side; photocopiable page 75 (one per child/pair);

Key vocabulary
total, balance, combination, strategy, solution

Brainteaser links
6: 'Cashing up' on page 13.
10: 'Shape mix' on page 14.

Activity introduction
● Present a demonstration set of number cards (see 'You will need'). Ask individuals to make a given target total using combinations of some of the cards. As the cards enable a maximum total of well over 100, target numbers can be as challenging as individual capability allows; disregard the number cards featuring the highest numbers if you want to work within a smaller range.
● Ask questions: *How would you make a total of 60? How did you work out what combination to use? What is the largest possible total? Are there any totals below that maximum which cannot be made?*
● If time allows, explain that the cards enable any whole number up to the maximum (127). If an extra card featuring 128 were included (that is, double 64), then the range would increase to 255.

Activity development
● Introduce an enlarged version of the balance scales featured on photocopiable page 75, but with a drawn mass on the left-hand side labelled 13. Next, present four similarly sized cards (labelled 1, 3, 7 and 16), explaining that these represent other masses. Ask the group if they can make the scales balance, using some or all of the four given masses. Unlike the group work above, it should soon be apparent that the cards cannot, on this particular occasion, be combined to give the required total. Allow children time to come up with the strategy of adding the mass labelled 3 to the left-hand side and counter-balancing on the right with the card labelled 16; if this strategy is not forthcoming you may need to demonstrate and set another similar challenge.
● Provide each child with photocopiable page 75, explaining that the mass on the left changes each time to give a different challenge.
● Ask questions: *How did you find the solution? Have you found all the different masses you could balance with just these four masses?*
● The second question on page 75 offers scope for further masses to be balanced.

Review
● Review the solutions, drawing out the strategies employed and guiding children towards a more systematic approach: for example, arranging all four masses on the right-hand side will balance 27 on the left; other masses can be balanced by losing or shifting masses from the right-hand side.

Next steps
● Ask the children to find other masses which could be balanced using the same four weights depicted throughout the photocopiable challenges.
● Modify the choice of masses to give similar challenges.

Name _____

In the balance

◀ Make the scales balance, using some or all of these masses.
Each mass may be used only once.

◀ What other masses could be balanced using some or all of the given masses?

Missing numbers

Learning objectives
(Y3) Calculate strand: Add or subtract mentally combinations of one-digit and two-digit numbers.
(Y4) Use/apply strand: Represent a problem using number sentences and diagrams; use these to solve the problem; present and interpret the solution in the context of the problem.

Expected prior knowledge
● Calculate rapidly differences between numbers to 20.

You will need
A set of 1-20 number cards; enlarged version of the ruler from photocopiable page 77; photocopiable page 77 (one per child).

Key vocabulary
difference, number sentence, solution, unit length, measurement, calculate

Brainteaser link
9: 'Full to the brim' on page 14.

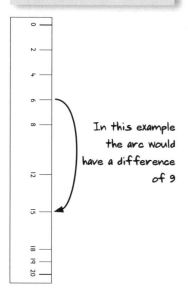

In this example the arc would have a difference of 9

Activity introduction
● Present a shuffled set of 1-20 number cards. Turn over the top card and place it face up in the centre of the table. Pass the pack to the first child who turns over the next card. The challenge is to find the difference between the two numbers before placing it over the first card. Continue passing the pack around, each time comparing the two cards before placing the new card over the central pack.
● Use this activity to talk about difference. Consider strategies for finding differences such as counting on from the smaller number, relating to similar calculations or using associated addition facts. Emphasise the fact that certain strategies work well in particular situations. For example, when finding the difference between 6 and 15 some children might consider the difference between 5 and 15 and then adjust using compensation.
● Ask questions: *How did you work it out? Could you give me a number sentence for that? Is difference the same as taking away? Are some calculations harder than others?*

Activity development
● Present an enlarged version of the ruler from photocopiable page 77, explaining that the ruler has lost some of its numbers. Select any two of the remaining numbers, such as 4 and 12, and ask how many units it is from one number to the other. Emphasise again the language of difference. Next, ask if there are any other points on the ruler which would give the same measurement (for example, a measurement from 0 to 8 is the same as a measurement from 4 to 12).
● Provide each child with photocopiable page 77 and ask them to find the three measurements given.
● As they work, identify whether there is any confusion or distortion of the task; reaffirm that you are looking for measurements based on the difference between any two of the given numbers.
● Stop the children as they approach the end of these initial challenges and consider how they might record their answers. Possible suggestions include number sentences, answers written in words, or possibly simple diagrams (see left).
● Ask questions: *How did you work out the answer? Is there more than one approach/strategy to find the answer?*
● Allow individuals to work on the last question on photocopiable page 77, which extends the task. Note that the ruler has been designed to enable every unit length from 1 to 20 to be created.

Review
● Review the solutions and the way they have been represented, identifying lengths for which there is more than one solution.

Next steps
● Ask the children to create a 0-10 ruler with which every unit length within the range can be measured. Challenge them to use as few markers as possible.

Name ______________________

Missing numbers

- How would you use this ruler to measure the following lengths?
- 3 units

____

____

- 16 units

____

____

- 9 units

____

____

- What other unit lengths can be measured with this ruler?

____

____

____

____

____

____

____

____

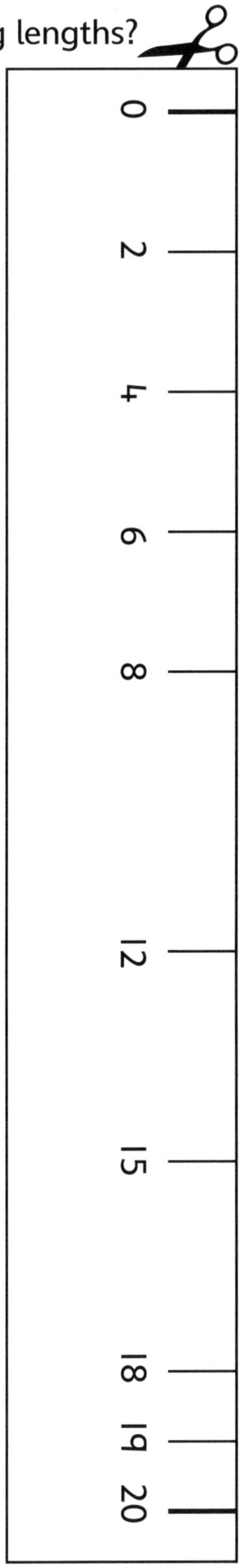
0
2
4
6
8
12
15
18
19
20

Magic circles

Learning objectives
(Y4) Use/apply strand:
Identify and use patterns, relationships and properties of numbers or shapes; investigate a statement involving numbers and test it with examples.
(Y4) Use/apply strand:
Report solutions to problems, giving explanations and reasoning orally and in writing.
(Y4) Calculate strand: Add or subtract mentally pairs of two-digit whole numbers (for example, 47 + 58, 91 - 35).

Expected prior knowledge
● Add several one-digit numbers reliably.

You will need
Enlarged copy of the number cards on photocopiable page 79; photocopiable page 79 (one per child); scissors (one pair per child).

Key vocabulary
sequence, strategy, total, equal, pattern, sub-total

Brainteaser link
14: 'Numbers up' on page 15.

Activity introduction
● Arrange an enlarged copy of the number cards on photocopiable page 79 in ascending order. Begin by adding the first number to the second number, recording the answer (9). Add this to the third number and continue to build a cumulative total (the final answer is 84). Ask children how they calculated the answers and share these strategies.
● Repeat the activity, this time inviting individual children to select 'convenient' numbers to add to the running totals. Adding 12 and 18, for example, is helpful because 30 is a multiple of 10. This could be added to the total of 21 and 9 for the same reason.
● Put the sequence back in ascending order and explore adding pairs of numbers, starting with the first number (3) and the seventh or last number (21), which gives 24. Then add the second number (6) to the sixth (18) and the third (9) to the fifth (15); each of these pairs also gives 24. The final step is to add the remaining number (12) to the three pair-totals of 24; ask children to suggest ways of doing this.

Activity development
● Provide each child with photocopiable page 79 and a pair of scissors. Explain the task as presented. Clarify that each circle will contain four numbers.
● Observe the children as they arrange the tiles across the diagram, noting the strategies they employ. Some children may work randomly initially, with some trial and improvement as they try to equalise the totals. Others may be more deliberate in their reasoning, beginning, for example, by placing the smallest number at the centre.
● Ask questions: *What strategy did you use to find a solution? Is there another way? Why does it balance? How did you add the numbers mentally?*
● Encourage early finishers to record their solution as a permanent record of achievement. Alternatively, ask them to find another solution (there are eight in total, one of which is shown below).

Review
● Discuss the solutions, including the way that small numbers are 'compensated' by larger numbers. Explore strategies such as placing the smallest/largest/middle number at the centre.
● Consider also how the inner numbers could be exchanged with the outer numbers to give different solutions.

Next steps
● Photocopiable page 79 can be made more/less challenging by changing the sequence to something other than the multiples of 3. The numbers used should always be the first seven multiples (for example, 5, 10, 15, 20, 25, 30, 35).

Magic circles

◼ Arrange one number tile in each space so that each circle has the same total.

◼ Are there other ways of arranging the numbers to achieve the same result?

| 3 | 6 | 9 | 12 | 15 | 18 | 21 |

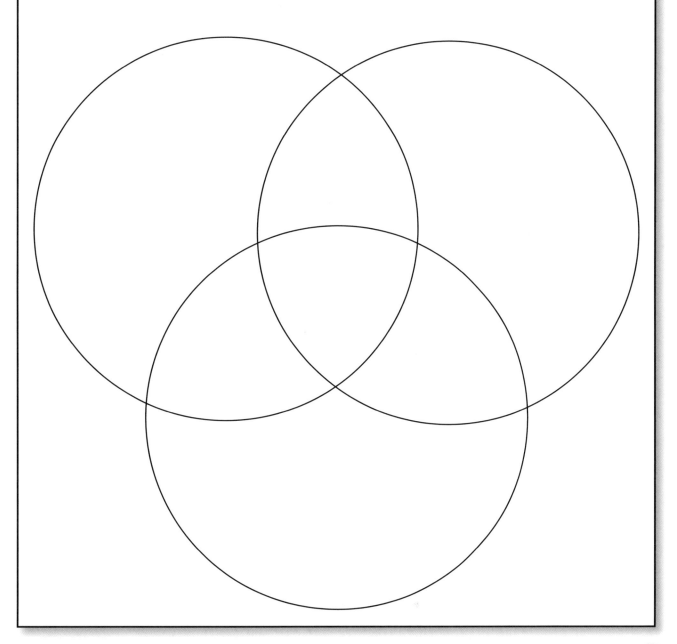

Shrinking squares

Learning objectives
(Y4) Use/apply strand:
Identify and use patterns, relationships and properties of numbers or shapes; investigate a statement involving numbers and test it with examples.
(Y4) Calculate strand:
Subtract mentally pairs of two-digit whole numbers (for example, 91 – 35).

Expected prior knowledge
● Derive differences without the routine need for written methods of calculation.

You will need
Large whiteboard; individual whiteboards; enlarged version of the shrinking square at the top of photocopiable page 81; photocopiable page 81 (one per child).

Key vocabulary
difference, pattern, reduce, adjacent, strategy

Activity introduction
● Present a two-digit number on a large whiteboard and generate a second number by finding the difference between the two digits. Now create a chain by calculating the difference between these two numbers. Continue to find differences between the last two numbers in this chain. This should create a finite chain of numbers which ultimately 'settles' at 0. For example:

$16 \rightarrow 5 \rightarrow 11 \rightarrow 6 \rightarrow 5 \rightarrow 1 \rightarrow 4 \rightarrow 3 \rightarrow 1 \rightarrow 2 \rightarrow 1 \rightarrow 1 \rightarrow 0$

● Discuss the strategies used for this calculation, including counting on from the lower number.
● Invite individuals to select a starting number of their own to see what happens in any chain. Give further opportunity for experimentation in pairs with individual whiteboards.
● Show the children an enlarged version of the shrinking square from the top half of photocopiable page 81. Model the process for solving shrinking squares: the difference between each pair of adjacent corner numbers is recorded along the four sides of the square; a new square is then created using the new numbers and the calculations are repeated; this process is followed until the numbers reduce to 0 (see example right).

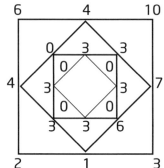

Activity development
● Provide each child with photocopiable page 81. Invite them to attempt the first shrinking square independently (if necessary, refer to your modelled example). Encourage them to try the second shrinking square for themselves, observing their progress throughout.
● As well as checking children's answers, try to ascertain the methods of calculation used and test their recall of associated number facts. You should also notice individuals beginning to realise that the numbers tend towards 0 with each progressive step.
● If children have difficulty with the spatial element of the grid pattern, you could provide a template of a grid with several shrinking squares.
● Ask questions: *What strategy did you use to calculate the difference between the pair of numbers? Is there another way? What do you notice? Will a shrinking square always work?*

Review
● Discuss the solutions and ask children why they think the numbers reduce to 0. Look at some of the patterns created by those who had time to try numbers of their own.
● Try an 'extreme' example where, for example, three corners are given a single digit and the remaining corner a number such as 100. Ask the children whether they think it will still work. (It does.)

Next steps
● Try some 'extreme' examples, as outlined in the Review session.

Shrinking squares

◢ Find the differences in the numbers at adjacent corners to solve these shrinking squares.

◢ Create your own shrinking square, using four corner numbers of your own. What happens?

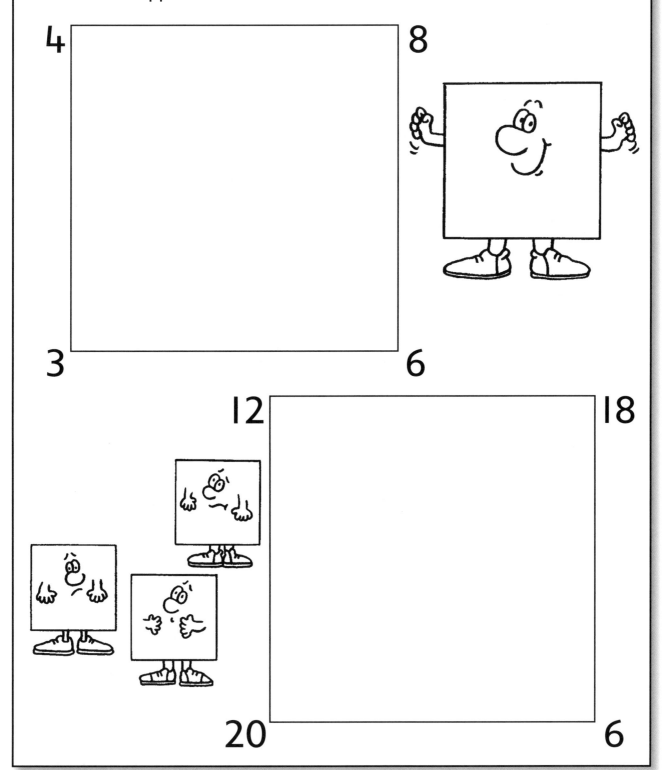

Words worth

Learning objectives
(Y4) Use/apply strand: Collect, organise and interpret selected information to find answers. **(Y4) Calculate strand:** Add or subtract mentally pairs of two-digit whole numbers (for example, 47 + 58, 91 - 35).

Expected prior knowledge
● Use mental and written methods efficiently to add several two-digit numbers.

You will need
Large whiteboard; photocopiable page 83 (one per child); individual whiteboards or paper.

Key vocabulary
pence, value, total, order, pairings, near double

Activity introduction
● Use a large whiteboard to present an enlarged version of this diagram:

| 12 | 17 | 23 | 18 |

● Discuss ways in which the total can be found, addressing a range of strategies, including adding 'convenient' pairs: for example, adding 18 and 17 gives a near double, adding 23 and 12 gives a multiple of 5. You could also add the tens digits first (as the most significant).
● Encourage individual children to declare what is their own preferred approach.
● If time allows, create a similar set of numbers to offer further practice of calculation strategies.

Activity development
● Provide copies of photocopiable page 83. Alternatively, print directly onto card and cut out the letters as playing cards. Introduce the idea of making a short word with the letters and guide children through the process of calculation to work out what the word is worth. Remind the group about the function of the magic card (which can be used as any letter). Reinforce the associative nature of addition, where the order of addition has no impact on the result.
● Observe the range of calculation strategies employed and ask questions in cases where these approaches are not apparent.
● Encourage the children to show their working where calculations involve written approaches. If you prefer, try to 'capture' some of these processes while the children make informal and temporary jottings on individual whiteboards.
● Encourage the children to collaborate in their choice of letters and the calculation of values. This will help to identify different results arising from careless or occasional errors.
● Ask questions: *In which order did you add the numbers? Were there any easy combinations? Can you make a longer word?*
● Children should enjoy the added challenge of finding a word which beats their own personal best.

Review
● Review the different scores achieved and re-establish the repertoire of addition strategies used.

Next steps
● Disregarding the letters, use the set of values to set some direct challenges of a typically closed nature (for example: *Show me two cards with a total of exactly 39p*). Invite the children to write some questions of their own, including some involving subtraction.
● Review the vocabulary specific to the activities covered in the session, especially that detailed above.

Words worth

■ Create some words using these letter cards.
■ Calculate how much each word is worth. (You can use the magic card as any letter.)

a	**s**	**t**	**e**
23p	31p	19p	11p
p	**o**	**m**	**d**
26p	14p	25p	21p
w	**r**	**g**	**any letter**
17p	20p	27p	18p

Magic arc

Learning objectives
(Y4) Use/apply strand:
Identify and use patterns,
relationships and properties
of numbers or shapes;
investigate a statement
involving numbers and test
it with examples.
(Y4) Use/apply strand:
Report solutions to
problems, giving
explanations and reasoning
orally and in writing.
(Y4) Calculate strand: Add
or subtract mentally pairs of
two-digit whole numbers
(for example, 47 + 58,
91 – 35).

Expected prior knowledge
● Add several single-digit
numbers reliably.

You will need
Enlarged set of 1–6 number
cards; photocopiable page
85 (one per child); scissors
(one pair per child).

Key vocabulary
sequence, arc, strategy,
total, equal, pattern, sub-
total

Activity introduction
● Present an enlarged set of 1-6 number cards. Having established that the sum of the digits is 21, try some quick-fire questions where two or more numbers need to be added to make totals below 21.
● Ask questions: *How did you add the numbers mentally? Is there another way?*
● Explain to the children that the skills they have used will serve them well in the task which follows.

Activity development
● Provide each child with photocopiable page 85 and a pair of scissors. Explain the task as presented. The task features the same numbers as in the introduction. Clarify that each of the three arcs takes in four numbers (the children may be unfamiliar with the word 'arc' in this context, and you may need to explain it).
● Observe the children arranging the numbers across the diagram, noting the strategies they employ. Some children may work randomly initially, with some trial and improvement as they try to equalise the totals. Others may be more deliberate in their reasoning, beginning, for example, by placing the smallest numbers at the three extremities of the puzzle.
● Ask questions: *What strategy did you use to find a solution? Is there another way? Why does it balance? How did you add the numbers mentally?*
● If it is considered helpful, the group can be given a target total of 14 for each arc.
● Encourage early finishers to record their solution as a permanent record of achievement. Alternatively, ask them to find another solution (there are several, four of which are shown below).

Solutions

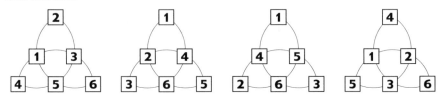

Review
● Discuss the solutions, including the way that smaller numbers are compensated by larger numbers. Explore strategies such as arranging the three smallest/largest/odd/even numbers in the central area.
● The sum of the digits is 21. As each number is used twice, the overall total is 42. In turn, each of the three arcs must share that total, so the total for each sum must be 14.

Next steps
● Photocopiable page 85 can be made more challenging by changing the sequence (for example, use 2, 4, 6, 8, 10, 12). Ask the children to predict how many different solutions they think there will be.

Magic arc

■ Arrange one number in each box so that each arc of four numbers has the same total.

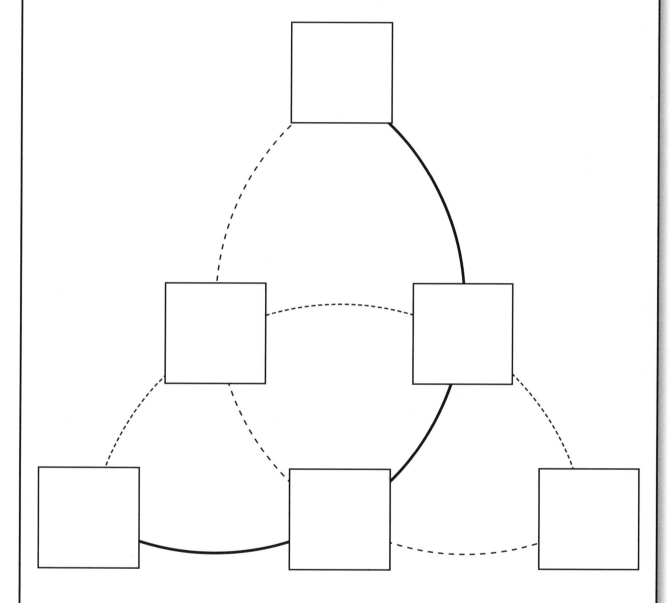

■ Are there other ways of arranging the numbers to achieve the same total?

| 1 | 2 | 3 | 4 | 5 | 6 |

Bits and pieces

Activity introduction
- Provide a set of 12 objects for counting and count these out on the table. Arrange the objects as a 4 by 3 array – this offers a strong visual model when dividing the set into smaller groups.
- Ask individual children to show you fractions of that set. Remind them of the need for each subset to be equal in number (for example, when dividing the set into quarters, each subset must have three objects in it).
- Begin with unit fractions such as $\frac{1}{4}$ before moving on to more complex fractions such as $\frac{2}{3}$. If required, explain that when the numerator is greater than 1 it is useful first to find the quantity associated with the relevant unit fraction (for example, $\frac{1}{4}$ of 12 is 3, so $\frac{3}{4}$ of 12 is 9).

Activity development
- Organise the children into pairs or small groups of up to four children. Provide them with the dice (see 'You will need') and one copy of photocopiable page 87 per child.
- Explain that turns are taken to roll the dice. The two outcomes are combined to form a question such as: What is $\frac{1}{4}$ of 8?
- If the answer to a question leads to a whole number answer, the child can record the dice outcomes and the answer on the chart. If the answer is not whole, the player records nothing for that turn.
- Play continues until all 12 rows are completed, after which the total of each child's answers is found. The winner is the player with the highest total.
- Ask questions such as: *How will you work that out? Do you think that will give a whole number answer?*
- Provide practical equipment such as cubes (if appropriate) and try to use some of the specific vocabulary (as detailed).

Review
- Develop the ideas explored in the activity introduction with a different number. Aim to work with other unit fractions, such as $\frac{1}{5}$, and see if the set of objects can be visualised rather than physically handled.
- If time allows, consider talking about fractions of quantities in the context of money. Begin with £1.00 and discuss the amounts equating to $\frac{1}{4}$, $\frac{3}{5}$, $\frac{2}{5}$ and so on.

Learning objectives
(Y4) Use/apply strand: Solve one-step and two-step problems involving numbers, money or measures, including time; choose and carry out appropriate calculations.
(Y4) Calculate strand: Find fractions of numbers, quantities or shapes (for example, $\frac{1}{5}$ of 50 plums $\frac{3}{8}$ of a 6 by 4 rectangle).

Expected prior knowledge
- Work with a range of unit fractions.
- Understand common fractions with numerators other than 1.

You will need
A set of 12 objects for counting; dice labelled $\frac{1}{2}$, $\frac{2}{3}$, $\frac{1}{3}$, $\frac{3}{4}$, $\frac{1}{4}$, $\frac{1}{6}$ and 2, 4, 6, 8, 10, 12 (one of each per pair or small group of up to four children); photocopiable sheet 87 (one per child); counting equipment such as cubes (optional).

Key vocabulary
fraction, whole number, remainder, divided by, equal groups, numerator, denominator

Brainteaser link
13: 'My perfect number' on page 15.

Next steps
- Modify the two dice to include more challenging fractions and numbers. Select numbers with enough factors to give a reasonable hit rate when played in a game situation.
- Begin to consider fractions of numbers where the answer is not an integer. Develop awareness of decimal notation by looking at such answers derived with a calculator.

Bits and pieces

This is a game for two or more players.
■ Use two special dice for this activity: one with fractions and one with multiples of 2.

Fraction	Amount	Answer

Maze

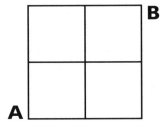

Activity introduction
- Present a large representation of the grid shown here. If each section is the length of a programmable vehicle, this can be used to model the task physically.
- Ask individual children to track a pathway from the corner marked A to that marked B. Encourage them to find all six different pathways, using terminology such as 'similar', 'turn', and 'right angle'.
- If time allows, consider doing a similar exercise with a 3 × 2 grid.

Activity development
- Provide copies of photocopiable page 89 and invite individuals to show some of the ways of tracking the word 'maze'. A successful track must contain all four letters in the correct order, either in a straight line or in a jagged manner. It is permissible to move only from one square to an adjacent square, and this rules out cases where the word is interrupted with a line break.
- Offer centimetre squared paper should children want to create identical arrays in which to record individual pathways.
- Set the challenge of trying to find all the possible pathways.
- If suitable attack strategies appear to be lacking, encourage the group to focus on just one of the cells (containing the letter M) at a time.
- Ask questions: *Where did you start? How many words can you make starting from just this cell? How many words do you think there will be?*

Review
- Go through both the methodology and the solution (16 different pathways in total). Although it is not the only approach, the strategy suggested earlier helps to break the task into smaller steps. The array shown here shows the number of ways in which the word can be made, in relation to the cells from which they start.

8			1
		3	
	3		
	1		

Next steps
- Create different arrays and/or make use of words of three to five letters in length.
- When undertaking related tasks, consider the use of compass directions as a method of describing movement about a grid. This would align the task more centrally with NPS objectives from Year 3 onwards.
- Reference to the solution given above reveals a diagonal line of 1, 3, 3, 1. This relates closely to Pascal's Triangle and is something which could be investigated.

Learning objectives
(Y3) Shape strand: Read and record the vocabulary of position, direction and movement, using the four compass directions to describe movement about a grid.
(Y4) Use/apply strand: Report solutions to problems, giving explanations and reasoning orally and in writing.

Expected prior knowledge
- Use the language of shape and line.
- Recognise and describe quarter turns and right angles.

You will need
Large 2 × 2 square grid; floor vehicle and prepared board (both optional); photocopiable page 89 (one per child); centimetre squared paper.

Key vocabulary
pathway, turn, right angle, straight, opposite, similar

Maze

■ How many different ways can you make the word 'maze'? All the letters must be in the correct order, and in adjacent squares.

M	A	Z	E	M
A	Z	E	M	A
Z	E	M	A	Z
E	M	A	Z	E

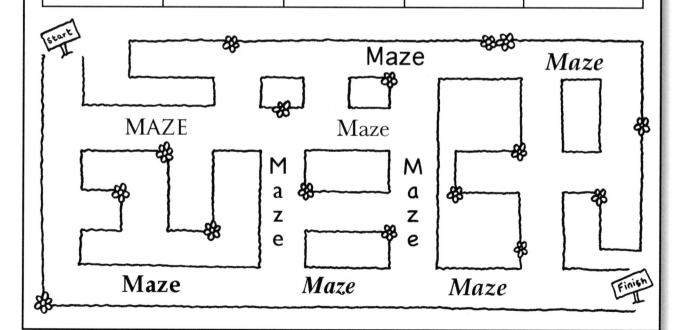

Triangle puzzle

Activity introduction

● Prepare a set of cards, to be shown in the following order:
1. What shape am I?
2. I am a two-dimensional shape.
3. I have four straight sides.
4. I have two pairs of parallel sides.
5. I am a regular shape.
6. I am a square.

● Introduce the first card, explaining to the children that they must guess the shape from the clues that follow. Begin by asking them to use individual whiteboards to draw any shape, including representations of solid shapes.

● Share ideas around the group, considering the names and properties of those drawn. The second card will focus attention on plane shapes alone, giving the children a chance to draw a different shape.

● After giving each piece of information, encourage them to refine their ideas (but don't disclose the actual shape until the final card is turned).

● In preparation for the individual work, you may want to discuss the word 'oblong', meaning a rectangle which is not a square.

Activity development

● Provide each child with photocopiable page 91 and a pair of scissors. Ask them to cut out the triangles from their sheet and attempt to make the shapes as requested. (The solution is given below left).

● Observe individuals to identify any differences in their spatial awareness and capability.

● Ask questions: *What are the essential properties of the (given) shape? What do these shapes have in common?*

● Use the stimulus question on the worksheet to identify whether the children appreciate that the area of each shape is the same.

Review

● If this has not yet featured in the discussion, consider precisely what defines a parallelogram (that is, it is a quadrilateral with two pairs of parallel sides). You might at this point establish that although we often think of a parallelogram as having no right angles, this is not a necessary condition. As such, a rectangle is a special-case parallelogram.

● Refer to the created triangle and discuss its properties. Point out that this triangle has a right angle and only two different side lengths. It is a right-angled isosceles triangle.

● Finally, sit one of the component triangles against a large, four-piece triangle. Orientate both in the same way to make the comparison more direct. Establish that the only mathematical property which differs is one of scale (size).

Learning objectives
(Y4) Use/apply strand: Identify and use patterns, relationships and properties of numbers or shapes.
(Y4) Shape strand: Draw polygons and classify them by identifying their properties.

Expected prior knowledge
● Recognise shapes and describe their properties.

You will need
Set of clue cards ; individual whiteboards; photocopiable page 91 (one per child); scissors (one pair per child).

Key vocabulary
two-dimensional shape, plane, solid, regular, parallel, edges, vertices, similar

Brainteaser link
16: 'What's in a name?' on page 16.

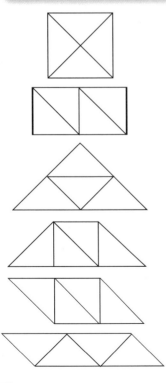

Next steps
● Create other shapes from four triangles.
● Use a copy of the classic Chinese tangram (see Lesson 33, Tangram puzzle). Once cut into its seven pieces, the jigsaw can be used as a vehicle to discuss shapes and their properties.

Triangle puzzle

■ Use four pieces each time to make a square, oblong, triangle, trapezium and parallelogram.

■ Which shape covers the largest area?

Tangram puzzle

Learning objectives
(Y4) Use/apply strand: Identify and use patterns, relationships and properties of numbers or shapes.
(Y4) Shape strand: Draw polygons and classify them by identifying their properties.

Expected prior knowledge
● Recognise the featured shapes and describe some of their properties.

You will need
Enlarged set of shapes from photocopiable page 93, labelled randomly from a–g; photocopiable page 93 (one per child); scissors (one pair per child).

Key vocabulary
similar, congruent, combination, equivalent, plane, parallel

Brainteaser link
16: 'What's in a name?' on page 16.

Activity introduction
● Arrange an enlarged set of shapes from photocopiable page 93, labelled a–g, across a table and invite the children to create some visual formulae where two or more pieces can be 'jigsawed' together to create a shape identical to one of the larger pieces.
● Let individual children test out their attempts. Record these as you would a number sentence (for example, c = b + f).
● Take every opportunity to use key shape vocabulary, including 'similar', 'congruent', 'combination' and 'equivalent'.

Activity development
● Provide each child with photocopiable page 93 and a pair of scissors. Ask them to cut out the shapes from the sheet. Encourage them to choose which of the three challenges they would like to tackle first as this will discourage the copying of solutions. When a solution is found, ask the child to sketch how it was created for future reference.
● The task of creating two congruent squares involves dividing the pieces into two smaller sets of shapes and is therefore probably the easiest problem to solve. After some early experimentation, the children should get a sense of how large each square is likely to be.
● Observe the children to see how they use trial and improvement to approximate each shape.
● This is quite a challenging task; for some children, it may be necessary to provide shape outlines for each of the three challenges.
● Ask questions: *What properties does this (given) shape have? Why are these differently sized triangles similar?*

Solutions

Review
● Discuss the solutions. If sketches have been kept along the way, use these to identify any variations between answers.
● Talk about the conservation of area between the large square and the triangle. Show the children that the large square can be divided into two triangles (across a diagonal) and that one of these 'halves' can be rotated about the other to create the large triangle.

Next steps
● Explore the additional suggested activity at the foot of page 93. This allows children an opportunity to create other shapes. Unless you want to use this as a 'free' activity, constrain the task by requiring the pieces to join along their sides (avoiding holes between the pieces).
● If not already discussed, look at the three different sizes of triangle. Establish that the scale is the only mathematical difference.
● Use an internet search engine to find historical and other mathematical links to the puzzle.

Tangram puzzle

■ Use all seven puzzle pieces each time to make the following shapes:
  a) A square
  b) A right-angled triangle
  c) Two congruent squares.

■ Make other shapes using some or all of the pieces.

Robots

Activity introduction

- Introduce the idea of growth and enlargement in a number context by repeatedly doubling a number; start at 1. Target individuals according to how difficult the particular double happens to be (for example, double 128 is made complex by the doubling of the units digit).
- Practise doubling sequences which begin with a single-digit number other than 1.
- Start with a high number and repeatedly halve.

Activity development

- Discuss making the classroom twice as big. Talk about how the room would be twice as long as well as being twice as wide. Encourage children to visualise the fact that the room would also be twice as high. At this stage, avoid any overt reference to the volume of the space being eight times greater, as this is an outcome of the lesson's development.
- Introduce photocopiable page 95. Allow each child or pair to make the robot and discuss its height, width and the total number of cubes. Invite them to estimate how many cubes they will need to make a similar robot which is twice as big.
- In a mathematical context the term 'similar' means 'having the same properties as the original in all features bar scale' (if the two robots were to be identical they would be 'congruent').
- Encourage individuals to make an estimate even if it becomes clear that this will prove incorrect. In some cases you may want to let the children revise their estimate as they progress through the task.
- Children will often begin by focusing solely on the vertical dimension. Try to steer the conversation to include the dimensions of width and depth.
- As the larger robot uses 48 cubes in total, you may find it more practical to encourage pairs to work together.
- Ask questions: *How many do you think you'll need? How do you know how tall to make your robot? How many cubes will you need to make just the robot's head?*
- Move on to the follow-up question on the photocopiable page, possibly imposing a limit of (say) ten cubes for the smaller animal.

Review

- Compare the animals made by the children, recording answers in a tabular form with two columns of figures for the original and enlarged models. Encourage the group to identify the connection between the columns (the number of cubes in the enlarged figure is the number of cubes in the original figure multiplied by 8).

Learning objectives
(Y3) Use/apply strand:
Represent the information in a problem, using numbers images or diagrams; use these to find a solution and present it in context.
(Y4) Shape strand:
Visualise 3D objects from 2D drawings; make nets of common solids.

Expected prior knowledge
- Understand and use some of the related vocabulary.

You will need
Photocopiable page 95 (one per child/pair); interlocking cubes (at least 48 per child/pair); squared and/or isometric paper (extension task only).

Key vocabulary
twice as big, enlargement, scale factor, multiple, how many?, pattern

Brainteaser link
14: 'Numbers up' on page 15.

Next steps
- Use squared paper to make 2D pictures and then enlarge them by scale factor 2 (or more).
- If visual perception is well developed, isometric paper could be used to create 2D representations of 3D objects made from cubes.

Robots

Make this simple robot with six cubes.

◼ Now make a robot twice as big. Before you start, write down how many cubes you estimate you will need to make the robot.

Estimate	Result
cubes	cubes

◼ Make a simple animal out of cubes and then make another twice as big.

Make that shape

Activity introduction

- Get the children to turn through quarter and half turns on the spot and refer to the angular measurement (as multiples of 90) in degrees.
- Introduce the idea of movement in between each turn to allow individuals to travel from one place to another.
- Consider asking one child to guide another to a fixed target position around the room.
- Begin to relate the measurement of turns to the properties of a simple shape such as a square.

Activity development

- Provide each individual or pair of children with photocopiable page 97 and a large sheet of paper (if using a programmable vehicle with a pen facility, the track will be recorded directly onto the sheet).
- Encourage an attempt of the more basic shapes initially as this will give some insights into the mathematics behind the angular measurement.
- Ask questions: *How much is a full turn in degrees? What fraction of a full turn are you going to calculate? How did/will you work out that answer?*
- For regular shapes each turn equates to 360/n, where n is the number of sides.
- The five-pointed star is a complex shape and it may be that an approximation of the angle of each turn offers sufficient challenge. For reference, the total turn is 720° (two full turns) made up of five turns of 144°. Alternatively, the angle of each point within the star can be calculated from the regular pentagon which lies at the heart of the shape.
- A common misconception is that the internal angle is the amount of turn required, when in fact it relates to the exterior angle.
- Most robots have a repeat facility which avoids the need to repeatedly enter the side length and measure of turn. You will need to refer to the user manual as procedures vary between models.

Review

- Revisit the vocabulary of movement and turn. If they have not been used previously, introduce the terms 'anti-clockwise' and 'clockwise'.

Learning objectives
(Y4) Use/apply strand: Suggest a line of enquiry and the strategy needed to follow it; collect, organise and interpret selected information to find answers.
(Y5) Shape strand: Use knowledge of properties to draw 2D shapes.
(Y5) Shape strand: Estimate, draw and measure acute and obtuse angles, using an angle measurer or protractor to a suitable degree of accuracy; calculate angles in a straight line.

Expected prior knowledge
- Recognise angle as a measurement of turn.
- Use the standard unit of degrees to represent a full or part turn.

You will need
Programmable vehicle with angle facility or screen-based software (if neither is available, the activity can be completed with rulers and protractors); photocopiable page 97 (one per child/pair); large sheets of paper.

Key vocabulary
polygon, triangle, pentagon, regular shape, angle, rotate, turn

Brainteaser link
16: 'What's in a name?' on page 16.

Next steps
- Investigate other polygons to reinforce the relationship between the number of sides and the angle of turn.
- Use a programmable robot to approximate a circle by repeatedly using a small side length and angle of turn.
- Develop the creation of a square by rotating the shape about one of its corners by a certain amount each time to make another shape; for example, drawing a series of small squares, each at 45° to the previous one, gives a large 'star', as shown here. Extend this method for other shapes.

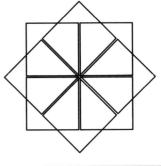

Make that shape

- Use a floor robot, screen robot or measuring equipment to create these different shapes.
- Think carefully about the measurement of each turn.

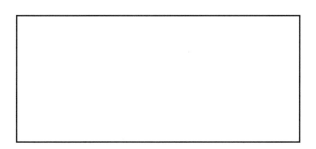

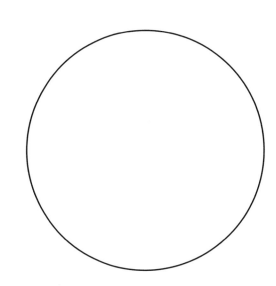

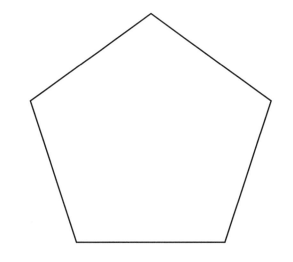

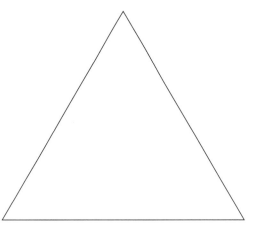

2D shape match

Activity introduction

Learning objectives
(Y4) Use/apply strand: Identify and use patterns, relationships and properties of numbers or shapes; investigate a statement involving numbers and test it with examples.
(Y4) Shape strand: Draw polygons and classify them by identifying their properties.

Expected prior knowledge
- Work with representations of plane shapes.
- Recognise the properties of shapes.
- Name some of the featured shapes.

You will need
Individual whiteboards; cards pre-cut from photocopiable page 99 (one set per pair); safety mirrors; mathematical dictionary.

Key vocabulary
polygon, triangle, square, pentagon, hexagon, heptagon, octagon, nonagon, decagon, undecagon, dodecagon, equilateral, right-angled, isosceles, scalene, regular, irregular

Brainteaser link
10: 'Shape mix' on page 14.

- Present the word 'polygon' and invite the children to suggest what it means. The two parts of the word stand for 'many sided' and 'plane shape'. You should add that a polygon is any closed, plane (flat) shape with straight sides.
- Invite the children to draw and name some flat shapes known to them, on individual whiteboards.
- Look at the range of polygons featured on photocopiable page 99, concentrating on those which are unlikely to be known. As the core task is initially about naming the shapes according to their number of sides, the key teaching point should relate to clues in the name (for example, 'undec' = 'ten and one more', 'dodec' = 'ten and two more' and so on). The names of shapes are detailed below for reference.

3 sides	Triangle		8 sides	Octagon
4 sides	Square		9 sides	Nonagon
5 sides	Pentagon		10 sides	Decagon
6 sides	Hexagon		11 sides	Undecagon
7 sides	Heptagon		12 sides	Dodecagon

- Ask questions: *What do we call this shape? Why can't we have a polygon with only two sides?*

Activity development

- Provide each pair of children with one set of cards pre-cut from photocopiable page 99. Arrange the cards (shuffled and face down) as a 4 × 5 array. The initial task is to play the game as 'pairs' (pelmanism).
- Players take turns to select two cards. The player must name the shape on each card. If they match, the player collects them both. If not, they are turned back over in their original position. Play continues until all ten pairs have been claimed, the winner being the player with the most cards.
- As a follow-up task, safety mirrors can be used to help the group identify and draw the lines of symmetry for each shape. As the shapes presented are all regular, the generalisation that a shape with n sides has n lines of symmetry can be established.

Review

- Look at the three other types of triangle (right-angled, isosceles and scalene). Demonstrate how some isosceles triangles also feature a right angle.

Next steps
- Encourage the children to explore the language of shape using internet search engines and mathematical dictionaries.
- Consider different types of quadrilaterals and discuss the necessary conditions for each one. A good mathematical dictionary is recommended for this, as some of the properties are very precise.

2D shape match

Match each shape to its name.

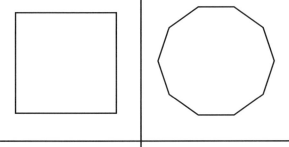 (square)	(decagon)	Pentagon	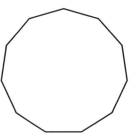
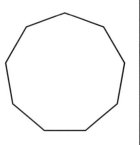	Heptagon	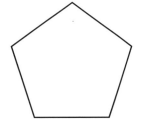	Triangle
Undecagon	(triangle)	Hexagon	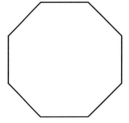
Octagon	Dodecagon	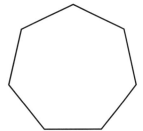	Decagon
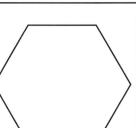	Square	Nonagon	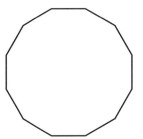

3D shape match

Learning objectives
(Y4) Use/apply strand: Identify and use patterns, relationships and properties of numbers or shapes.
(Y4) Shape strand: Draw polygons and classify them by identifying their properties.

Expected prior knowledge
● Work with representations of solid shapes.
● Recognise the properties of shapes.
● Name some of the featured shapes.

You will need
Cards pre-cut from photocopiable page 101 (one set per pair); construction materials; modelling clay (or similar); mathematical dictionary.

Key vocabulary
plane of symmetry, cube, cuboid, pentagonal, hexagonal, octagonal, prism, pyramid, icosahedron, dodecahedron

Activity introduction
● Present the word 'polyhedron' and invite the children to suggest what this means. The two parts of the word mean 'many sided' and 'solid shape'. You should add that a polyhedron is any closed, solid shape with flat faces.
● Invite the children to construct and name some simple solid shapes known to them.
● Look at the range of shapes represented on photocopiable page 101, concentrating on those which are unlikely to be known. The core task is initially about naming the shapes according to their number of faces and other key features (for example, a prism has a constant cross-section throughout its length). The names for each shape are listed in the grid shown here.
● Ask questions: *What do we call this shape? Why can't we have a polyhedron with three faces?*
● Look at the parallels between the names of 2D and 3D shapes (for example, dodecagon and dodecahedron are both derived from 'ten and two more').

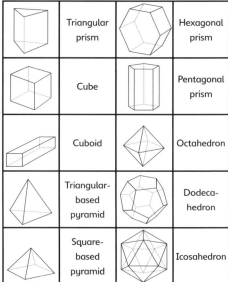

	Triangular prism		Hexagonal prism
	Cube		Pentagonal prism
	Cuboid		Octahedron
	Triangular-based pyramid		Dodeca-hedron
	Square-based pyramid		Icosahedron

Activity development
● Provide each pair of children with one set of cards pre-cut from photocopiable page 101. Arrange the cards (shuffled and face down) as a 4 × 5 array. The initial task is to play the game as 'pairs' (pelmanism).
● Players take turns to select two cards. The player must name the shape on each card. If the cards match, the player collects them both. If not, they are turned back over in their original position. Play continues until all ten pairs have been claimed, the winner being the player with the most cards.
● As a follow-up task, construction materials can be used to recreate all the featured solids. At this point you may want to talk about the shapes with symmetrical properties. As such shapes require a plane of symmetry (as opposed to a line) it may not be practicable to demonstrate other than by visualising the effect of a 'chop' in the appropriate area. To fully demonstrate this quality, some modelling clay or similar would be a valuable visual aid.

Review
● Reinforce the distinction between the pyramids and prisms.

Next steps
● Encourage the children to explore the language of shape using internet search engines and mathematical dictionaries.
● Explore the nets of some of the featured shapes.

Name _____

3D shape match

◼ Match each shape to its name.

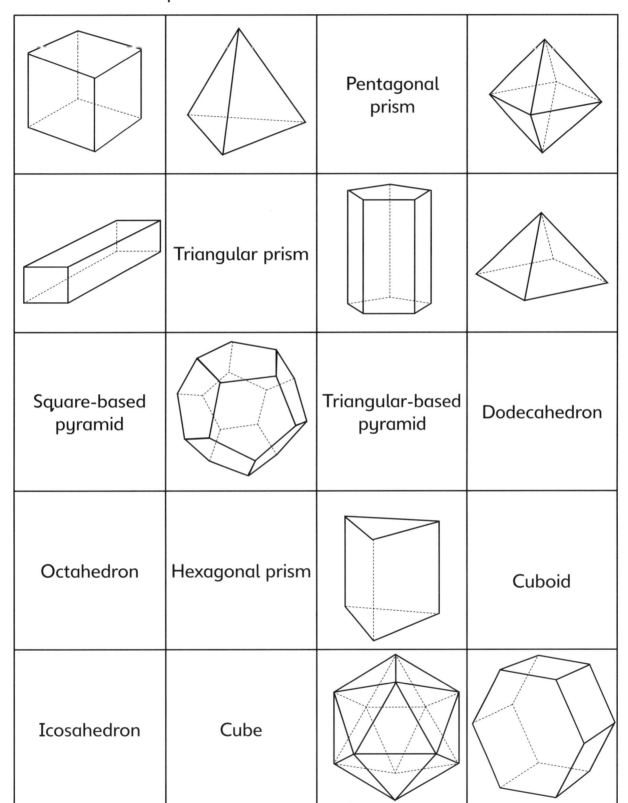

		Pentagonal prism	
	Triangular prism		
Square-based pyramid		Triangular-based pyramid	Dodecahedron
Octahedron	Hexagonal prism		Cuboid
Icosahedron	Cube		

What's in a shape?

Learning objectives
(Y4) Use/apply strand:
Suggest a line of enquiry and the strategy needed to follow it; collect, organise and interpret selected information to find answers.
(Y4) Use/apply strand:
Identify and use patterns, relationships and properties of numbers or shapes; investigate a statement involving numbers and test it with examples.
(Y5) Shape strand: Identify, visualise and describe properties of rectangles, triangles, regular polygons and 3D solids.

Expected prior knowledge
• Recognise common 3D shapes and talk about some of their properties.

You will need
3D solid shapes; photocopiable page 103 (one per child/pair); stock of construction materials for 3D shapes (can be solid pieces or frameworks).

Key vocabulary
tetrahedron, edges, faces, vertex, vertices, prism, pyramid, pattern, relationship, formula

Activity introduction
• Use a set of 3D shapes to revise the names of common examples. If children have prior experience of the concept of regularity in 2D geometry, the term can be applied to 3D examples such as the cube and tetrahedron where all the component faces are the same.
• Ask the group to identify any objects in everyday life which match the shapes demonstrated.

Activity development
• Present a completed model of a shape not featured on photocopiable page 103 (for example, a square-based pyramid). Encourage the children to visualise going inside the shape. Ask: *What would you see inside?*
• Ask other questions: *How many faces does the shape have?* (5) *How many vertices?* (5) *How many edges?* (8).
• Reinforce the idea of data collection by recording children's answers.
• Provide each child or pair of children with a copy of photocopiable page 103 and a wide selection of materials for construction (for example, Polydron).
• As particular shapes are investigated, encourage the children to create a table of results (see completed answer table below).
• Ask questions: *Do you think that shape will have more faces than this one? Will this shape have more edges than faces? How did you get that answer?*
• Invite the children to make predictions of their outcomes and focus on the inter-related nature of the results within each example.

Solution

	Edges	Vertices	Faces
Tetrahedron	6	4	4
Cube	12	8	6
Dodecahedron	30	20	12
Hexagonal prism	18	12	8

Review
• The idea that the total of the faces and the vertices is 2 more than the number of edges is attributed to the mathematician Euler. Some children may be able to follow the formula, which abbreviates the relationship as $F + V = E + 2$.
• Establish whether the group can clearly distinguish between a pyramid and a prism in terms of their mathematical properties. A prism is created when a polygon is represented consistently throughout the cross-section of a solid shape (with no change in its size). In contrast, a pyramid is formed when edges, projected from the vertices of the base, meet at a single point.

Next steps
• Use an internet search engine to find out more about Euler. Look at the work of other great mathematicians.
• Explore a wider range of polyhedra to establish that this relationship (Euler's rule) can be sustained.

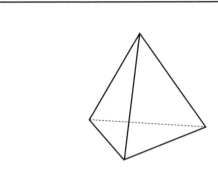

What's in a shape?

◼ Make each one of these 3D shapes with construction materials.

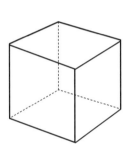
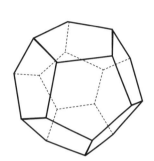
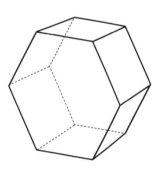

◼ Record the number of vertices, edges and faces in a table.

	Edges	**Vertices**	**Faces**
Tetrahedron			
Cube			
Dodecahedron			
Hexagonal prism			

◼ Look at the table. Can you find a pattern in your answers?

_____

_____

On reflection

Learning objectives
(Y3) Shape strand: Draw and complete shapes with reflective symmetry; draw the reflection of a shape in a mirror line along one side.
(Y4) Use/apply strand: Represent a problem, using number sentences, statements or diagrams; use these to solve the problem; present and interpret the solution in the context of the problem.

Expected prior knowledge
● Recognise shapes with properties of reflective symmetry.

You will need
Interlocking cubes (six per child); safety mirrors; photocopiable page 105 (one per child/pair); squared paper.

Key vocabulary
mirror line, symmetry, reflection, rotation, same, different

Activity introduction
● Provide each child with four interlocking cubes and a safety mirror. Ask them to produce a symmetrical image, where each piece lies flat on the surface and is joined by at least one other cube.
● Compare and contrast different arrangements, establishing that there are just three options (a stick, a square and a T-shape).
● Confirm that the group appreciates that the task is not simply about halving a set of cubes with a mirror, but about the image seen in the mirror being identical to the arrangement which lies beyond.

Activity development
● Provide each child or pair of children with photocopiable page 105 and two more cubes. Explain that the task is simply an extension of the four-cube problem already tackled.
● When working with pairs, encourage the children to alternate between creating a solution and recording the result. Impose a 'no-interference' rule so that each child has an opportunity to experiment.
● Ask questions: *Why is that shape the same as one you have already created? What will you try next? What would happen if you moved just that one piece to a different position?*
● Ask the children to record a 2D image of each of their shapes showing the line of symmetry (either on the photocopiable page or squared paper). The ten solutions are shown below. The two arrangements which are often overlooked feature mirror lines which cut across cubes rather than along an edge.

Solutions

Review
● Review the solutions and then explore arrangements of six cubes where they are allowed to be constructed with height; these shapes must be described as having planes, rather than lines, of symmetry.
● Explore the number of lines of symmetry within regular shapes (such as a square).
● Discuss the number of lines of symmetry in a circle (you might find it helpful to model the problem by folding a paper circle). Can the children begin to appreciate the notion of an infinite number of possibilities?

Next steps
● Explore reflections of a regular shape (such as a pentagon) where the mirror is placed within, along one side, touching at a corner or at a distance. Record some of the images thus created.
● Explore what happens to a shape when it is rotated about its centre, corner, mid-point of an edge, and so on. Mark the shape's track at staggered intervals to capture its movement.

Name _____

On reflection

◧ These six cubes give a symmetrical outline.

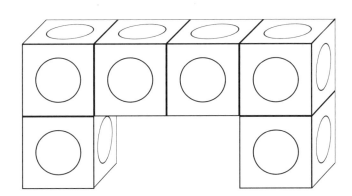 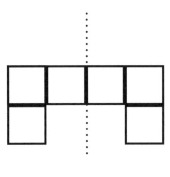

◧ Can you find nine more symmetrical shapes using six cubes each time?

◧ Draw your shapes in 2D and show their line of symmetry.

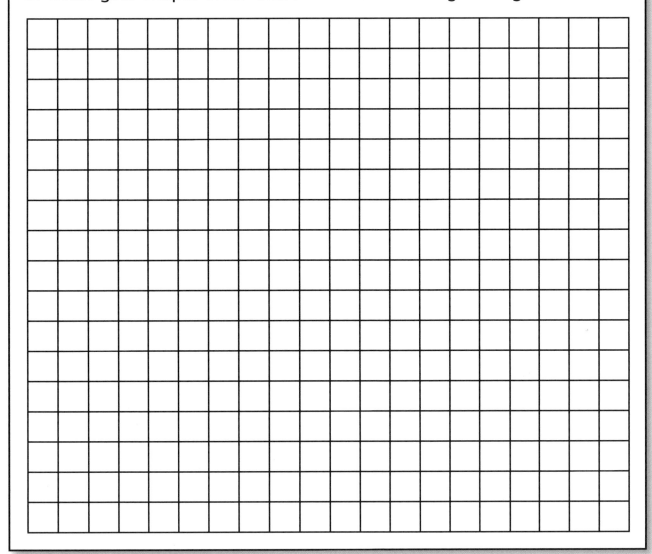

Take five cubes

Learning objectives
(Y3) Shape strand: Relate 2D shapes and 3D solids to drawings of them; describe, visualise, classify, draw and make the shapes.
(Y4) Use/apply strand: Represent a problem, using number sentences, statements or diagrams; use these to solve the problem; present and interpret the solution in the context of the problem.

Expected prior knowledge
● Recognise and perform rotations (turns) and reflections (flips).

You will need
Interlocking cubes (five per child); photocopiable page 107 (one per child/pair).

Key vocabulary
different, arrangement, rotation, reflection, puzzle, solution

Brainteaser link
20: 'Seeing spots' on page 17.

Activity introduction
● Ask the group to make shapes with four interlocking cubes, where each piece lies flat on the surface and is joined by at least one other cube.
● Compare different arrangements, ruling out those which are simply rotations or reflections of others. Establish that there are just four such arrangements possible (a stick, a square, an L-shape and a T-shape).

Activity development
● Provide each child or pair of children with a copy of photocopiable page 107. Explain that the task is simply an extension of the four-cube problem already tackled in the activity introduction.
● Observe which children are readily able to visualise and create different configurations. Listen in to conversations in order to gain some appreciation of their precision in language.
● When working with pairs, encourage them to alternate between creating a solution and recording the result. Impose a 'no-interference' rule so that each child has opportunity to experiment.
● Ask questions: *Why is that shape the same as one you have already created? What will you try next? What would happen if you moved just that one piece to a different position?*
● If one or two shapes prove to be elusive, encourage communication across the groups. All possible shapes are shown below.

Solution

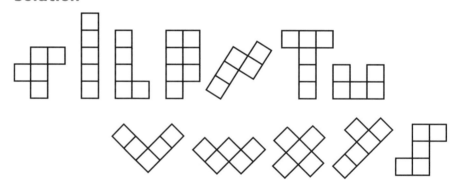

Review
● Review the solutions and find any missing shapes as a group. Although finding all the solutions is simply a matter of perseverance, it is possible to be methodical in the sense of modifying successful solutions slightly in order to generate new ones.

Next steps
● Challenge the group to work together to create a rectangle using the 12 shapes created in the activity (the 6 × 10 rectangle shown left is just one of over 2000 solutions). If the puzzle proves difficult, consider fixing the position of (say) half of the pieces.
● Use an internet search engine to find out more about the five-piece puzzle (the term 'pentominoes' is an effective keyword to use). Some activities will typically extend well beyond the capability of the group but some puzzles are intrinsically interesting.

Take five cubes

Five cubes can be joined together like this to give the shape below.

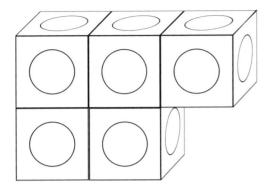 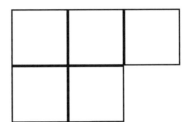

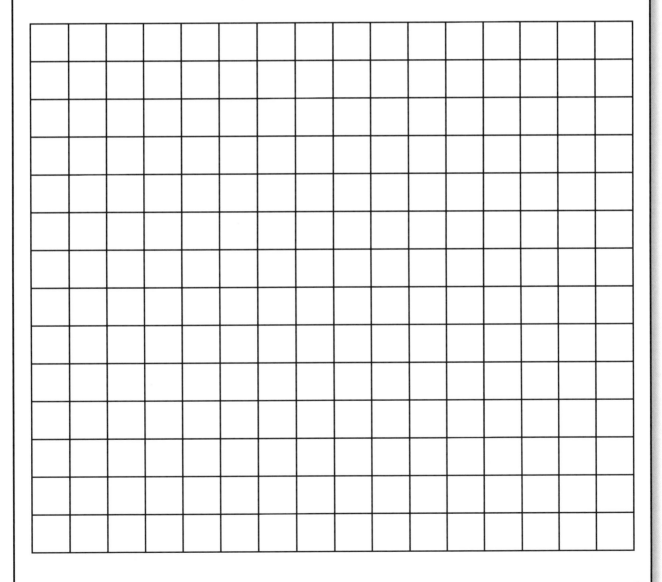

◼ Find all 12 different ways to join the five cubes together. Reflections and rotations do not count!

Scaled down

Learning objectives
(Y4) Use/apply strand:
Suggest a line of enquiry and the strategy needed to follow it; collect, organise and interpret selected information to find answers.
(Y4) Measure strand:
Choose and use standard metric units and their abbreviations when estimating, measuring and recording length, weight and capacity.

Expected prior knowledge
● Use strategies such as halving and doubling.
● Measure using the scale of a ruler.

You will need
Photocopiable page 109 (one per group); a range of standard and non-standard measuring equipment; calculators.

Key vocabulary
scale, halving, doubling, measurement, estimate

Brainteaser link
17: Made to measure' on page 16.

Activity introduction
● Practise doubling by beginning with a single-digit number and asking for its double, then continuing to double the answer.
● Ask questions: *How far can you go? How did you work that out?*
● Practise halving by beginning with a large multiple of 8 and encouraging children to halve that number repeatedly until one-eighth of the original number is found.

Activity development
● Provide one copy of photocopiable page 109 per small group of up to four children.
● Explain that equipment is available for the children to take the measurements required. Confirm that calculators are allowed to aid calculation when scaling down. Some 'rounding off' of numbers may be required.
● Once the children are clear about what 'one-eighth scale' means, observe how they establish its meaning in the context of this activity.
● The photocopiable page should have ample space for fitting in a full-length representation of a typical middle primary child.
● Ask questions: *What equipment will you use? Where will you start? How will you scale that answer down?*
● Those finishing early can add detail such as features. Again, much of this can be done through careful measurement.

Review
● Share the recorded outcomes of the exercise.
● Look at the range of measuring equipment used. Consider other equipment which might have been used.
● Look at the ratios within the human body (for example, what fraction of a person's height is taken up by the head?).
● Revise the equivalence between units of measurement (for example, 10mm = 1cm).

Next steps
● Look for further opportunities to consider reduction by different ratios.
● Consider the potential for scaling up measurements (for example, use a story about a giant as a starting point for creating representations of spectacles, toothbrushes and so on with a known enlargement factor).
● Research references to the so-called Golden Ratio, which suggests a universal notion of beauty through proportion. It is suggested that such notions are represented not only in the human form, but also in classic architecture and in other natural forms. There is a wealth of material on the internet.

Scaled down

■ Use measuring equipment to make a one-eighth scale picture of someone alongside this ruler.

■ Take measurements such as arm length and shoulder width to help you.

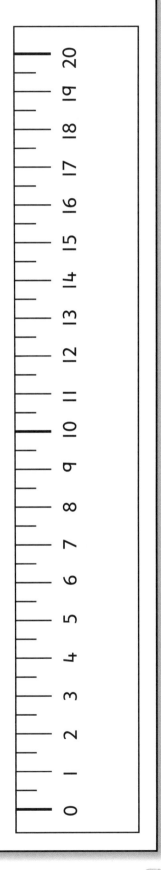

Round the block

Learning objectives
(Y4) Use/apply strand: Suggest a line of enquiry and the strategy needed to follow it; collect, organise and interpret selected information to find answers. **(Y4) Measure strand:** Draw rectangles and measure and calculate their perimeters; find the area of rectilinear shapes drawn on a square grid by counting squares.

Expected prior knowledge
● Understand and use the terms 'area' and 'perimeter'.

You will need
Pegboards (with, for example, 16 pins) and elastic bands (one per child/small group); photocopiable page 111 (one copy per child); interlocking cubes (12 per child); 2cm squared paper (optional).

Key vocabulary
perimeter, unit length, area, more, greater than, maximum, minimum

Brainteaser link
17: Made to measure' on page 16.

Activity introduction
● Provide pegboards and elastic bands and ask individuals to make rectangles of specific sizes (for example, 2 × 3). For each rectangle, establish that the group can calculate the area (by counting squares) and the perimeter (by counting unit lengths).
● Ask questions: *Does this shape have a different perimeter from the last shape? What is the smallest rectangle you can make?*
● Consider creating some irregular shapes and finding the area and perimeter in each case. Avoid making shapes which cross squares (diagonals) as the length of such a line is greater than a single unit ($\sqrt{2}$ to be precise).

Activity development
● Provide each child with photocopiable page 111 and 12 interlocking cubes.
● Ask the children to use all 12 cubes to create a rectangular array. Ask each child to tell the group the perimeter of the shape (establish the perimeter of the given shape, making sure that the children do not simply count a 'long side' as one unit). Assuming that differently proportioned rectangles are created, there should be more than one answer.
● Move on by asking the group to make an irregular shape, making sure the cubes are arranged as a flat construction. Again, ascertain that the perimeter can vary.
● Encourage the children to work individually, making a construction and recording the perimeter.
● The cubes could be arranged on 2cm squared paper or simply represented directly on the grid on photocopiable page 111.
● Ask questions: *What was the area of your shape?* (This is the same for all shapes.) *What was the perimeter? Can you make a shape with a larger perimeter? What is the maximum/minimum perimeter you can make?*

Review
● Show the children a representation of a 12 × 1 arrangement and establish that the perimeter is 26cm. Ask them to visualise a rectangle created by splitting that shape down its length and joining the ends together (forming a 24 × 0.5 rectangle). Establish that, while the area remains the same, the perimeter is significantly increased. What would happen to the perimeter if this process were repeated? (It would ultimately tend towards infinity!)

Next steps
● Consider activities where the perimeter of a shape is fixed to (say) 24 units. Encourage children to make a range of shapes, noting how the area changes. The most able children can be challenged to find the shape with the largest area (if the perimeter is 24 units, this is a 6 × 6 square).

Round the block

- This is a flat shape made using 12 cubes.
- Make some more flat shapes using 12 cubes.
- What is the perimeter of each shape?

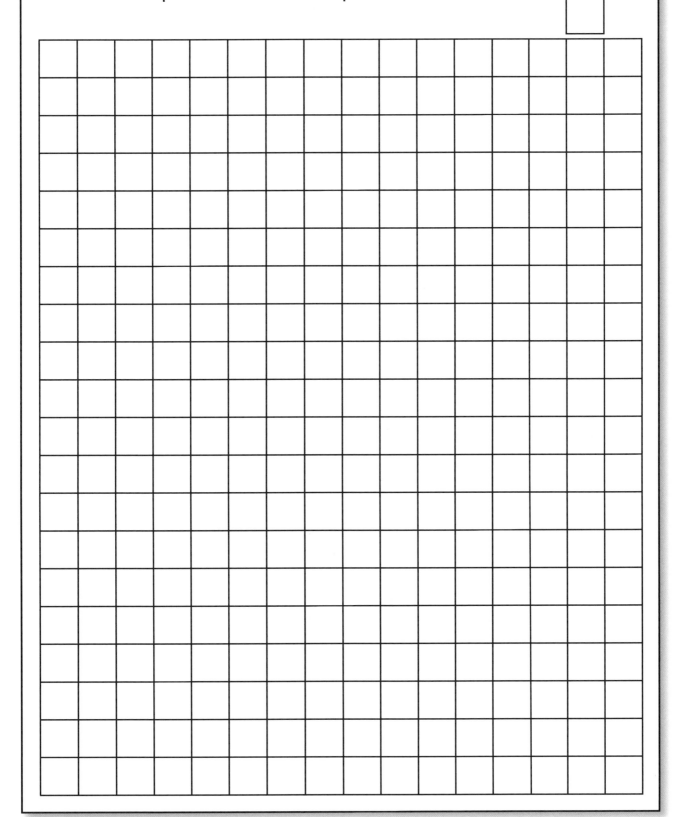

Measure for measure

Learning objectives
(Y5) Use/apply strand: Plan and pursue an enquiry; present evidence by collecting, organising and interpreting information.
(Y5) Measure strand: Read, choose, use and record standard metric units to estimate and measure length, weight and capacity; convert larger to smaller units, using decimals to one place (for example, change 2.6kg to 2600g).

Expected prior knowledge
● Recognise and use common units of measure, with a reasonable appreciation of the quantities one litre and one kilogram.

You will need
Various food/drink containers similar (but not necessarily identical) to those featured on photocopiable page 113; photocopiable page 113 (one per child); scissors (one pair per child).

Key vocabulary
millilitre, capacity, mass, more/less, unit of measure, pints, litres, kilogram

Brainteaser link
17: 'Made to measure' on page 16.

Activity introduction
● Engage the children in looking at the labelling of packaged food and drinks. Focus their attention on the units of measure featured.
● Remind them of the standard unit for capacity, passing round a 1 litre bottle.
● See if they can use this as a benchmark to make sense of the units displayed on smaller containers.
● Some units will be less familiar (for example, many European countries label products such as wine in centilitres (cl), where 1cl = 10ml).
● Establish a general distinction between units of measure for liquid and dry products but be prepared for certain anomalies (for example, some liquid products are now labelled in terms of their mass rather than their capacity).

Activity development
● Provide each child with photocopiable page 113 and a pair of scissors. The task is to cut out the individual cards and match each picture with the appropriate measurement. As there are variations in the size of food packages, there may be more than one acceptable solution. You should establish whether the matched items are reasonable in the context of the problem.
● Ask questions: *What units of measure does this have? What fraction is that of 1000 (ml)? What amount of juice do you estimate this will hold?*
● Alert the children to the use of imperial measures which still remain for products such as milk. At this point you could offer the conversion of 1 litre = 1.75 pints.
● The task could be extended by asking children to add drawings and measures of other practical items explored earlier in the lesson introduction.

Review
● Look at a relatively small container and ask related questions about measures in real contexts. For example: *How many of these juice cartons would I need if I wanted 1 litre of juice?*

Next steps
● Extend children's awareness of those imperial measures which are still in use and their metric conversions (for example, 1kg = 2.2 pounds).
● Develop some appreciation of larger units of measure (for example, 1 metric tonne = 1000kg). As a guide, the mass of a small car is now typically just a little over a metric tonne.
● At an appropriate point the relationship between mass and capacity can be explored (for example, 1 litre of water has a mass of 1 kilogram).

Measure for measure

0.5l	**5g**	**330ml**

1kg	**2l**	**4 pints**

75cl	**454g**	**100ml**

30g	**0.25l**	**80g**

Time for mathematics

Learning objectives
(Y4) Use/apply strand: Solve one-step and two-step problems involving numbers, money or measures, including time; choose and carry out appropriate calculations.
(Y4) Measure strand: Read time to the nearest minute; use am, pm and 12-hour clock notation; calculate time intervals from clocks and timetables.

Expected prior knowledge
● Tell the time (standard clock face).
● Understand and use the abbreviations am and pm.

You will need
Geared clock; photocopiable page 115 (one per child); scissors (one pair per child).

Key vocabulary
time, clock, digital, 24-hour clock, morning, afternoon, time difference, convert, timetable, outward journey, return journey

Brainteaser link
18: 'Something about me' on page 17.

Activity introduction
● Take the children through 24 hours using a geared clock to punctuate the day. Begin at 12 o'clock, explaining that you mean midnight. Roll the clock forward several hours, stopping routinely to ask about key events at those times.
● Stop at midday to ascertain the passage of 12 hours, using this to explain the rationale for the 24-hour clock times. Continue through to midnight.
● Teach conversion techniques (for example 17.00 hrs is 12 + 5 hours, so is the same as 5.00pm).
● Ask questions involving conversion to/from the 24-hour clock and align these with the analogue layout of the clock face.

Activity development
● Provide each child with a copy of photocopiable page 115. Ask them to cut out the cards. The task is to group the set of cards into clusters of three where the times are equivalent. Each of the three representational styles of time is quite distinctive, so you should be able to see at a glance if children are working along the right lines.
● Ask questions: *How will you convert that 24 hour time back to the 12 hour clock? This clock face shows half past so what will you be looking for on the digital time?*
● As a supplementary task, ask the children to suggest what they might be doing at each of the eight times (in words or pictures).

Review
● This section of the lesson assesses children's ability to convert to/from 24-hour clock times. Provide the group with a version of the train timetable below, which shows realistic data for planning a rail journey between Birmingham and London.

Birmingham (New Street) – London (Euston)						
		Choice 1	**Choice 2**	**Choice 3**	**Choice 4**
Outward journey	depart	11.30	12:00	12:30	13:00
	arrive	12:59	13:33	13:59	14:32
Return journey	depart	17:10	17:17	17:40	17:51
	arrive	18:39	18:56	19:09	19:27

● Establish whether the group can make sense of the timetable format, including the idea of different choices and the associated vocabulary.
● Ask questions: *Approximately how long does it take a train to get from Birmingham to London? What would be the latest train you could catch from Birmingham if you needed to get to London before 2.00pm? If you could get to Euston Station by 5.00pm, at what time would your train get you to Birmingham?*

Next steps
● Use timetables to calculate time differences (such as journey times).

Name _____

Time for mathematics

■ Group the cards into clusters of three, based on equivalent times.

20.30 hrs		10.35 hrs	8.30pm
7.30am	21.45 hrs		5.00pm
	12.00 hrs		15.15 hrs
	08.50 hrs	07.30 hrs	
9.45pm		8.50am	10.35am
3.15pm		17.00 hrs	12 noon

Made to measure

Learning objectives
(Y4) Use/apply strand: Suggest a line of enquiry and the strategy needed to follow it; collect, organise and interpret selected information to find answers.
(Y5) Measure strand: Read, choose, use and record standard metric units to estimate and measure length, weight and capacity to a suitable degree of accuracy (for example, the nearest centimetre).

Expected prior knowledge
● Obtain information from non-fiction texts and/or internet search engines.
● Use a calculator and interpret/convert the displayed information.

You will need
A selection of measuring instruments; real coins; photocopiable page 117 (one per child); calculators.

Key vocabulary
estimate, predict, measure, calculate, roughly

Brainteaser link
18: 'Something about me' on page 17.

Activity introduction
● Ask questions relating to aspects of measure: *How would you measure your height/weight? When might we use an angle measurer? What do we mean by area? How fast does a car travel and what does that mean?*
● You may have access to measuring instruments most typically used by upper primary pupils, such as micrometers, feeler gauges, internal/external callipers, trundle wheels, clinometers (for surveying) and depth gauges. Present these one at the time to establish whether any of the children have experience of such equipment.
● Once the use of the measuring instruments has been clarified, set some specific tasks to give a working knowledge of their application in real contexts (for example, measuring the length and width of the playground).

Activity development
● Photocopiable page 117 can be provided in the format given, or cut up and stapled to form a booklet of activities.
● The tasks do not necessarily require any of the measuring equipment used in the activity introduction; no equipment (other than calculators) is essential.
● Encourage the children to work in pairs (or groups of three) and begin by writing down some plans of action. These can be recorded alongside the tasks themselves, with agreed plans being approved or rejected by you.
● Use your judgement to decide whether potentially flawed approaches should be allowed to proceed. If necessary, remind the group of the availability of factual information in the library and via the internet.
● Encourage approximation as a technique for achieving a reasoned appreciation of the results. Done well, approximation can also act as a useful check on whether an answer is of the correct order.

Review
● Use this time as an opportunity to share results, comparing different approaches, and to focus on the units of measurement.
● Conclude by rehearsing the conversion of units of measurement. For example, clarify the conversion from mm to cm, cm to m, and m to km. Use these number sentences to establish, for example, how many millimetres must therefore equate to one metre. Some children may like the fact that a millimetre is actually one millionth of a kilometre.

Next steps
● Consider opportunities to measure and record units, including measurements to two decimal places (such as 1.26m).

Made to measure

◖How much would your height in pound coins be worth?

◖How many pound coins would be needed to balance your mass?

◖ How long would it take to walk to the moon?

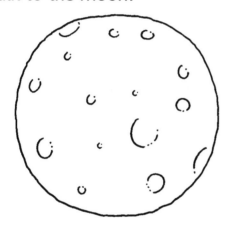

◖ How many footsteps in a mile?

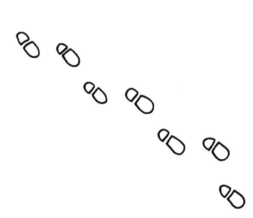

◖ Stretch out your arms. Is that wider than your own height?

Flags

Learning objectives
(Y3) Data strand: Answer a question by collecting, organising and interpreting data.
(Y4) Use/apply strand: Suggest a line of enquiry and the strategy needed to follow it; collect, organise and interpret selected information to find answers.

Expected prior knowledge
● Rapid recall of bonds to 12.

You will need
Photocopiable page 119 (one per child); two large dice; coloured pens/pencils (three colours per child).

Key vocabulary
problem, strategy, opposite, combination, different

Brainteaser link
19: 'In the mix' on page 17.
20: 'Seeing spots' on page 17.

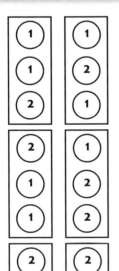

Activity introduction
● Roll two dice and add the numbers together. Talk about combinations. When any outcome is attained, ask for other ways that the same total might be achieved.
● Begin to establish that for some of the lower and higher totals (for example, 3 and 11), the number of dice combinations is restricted.
● Ask questions: *What dice total is most likely to come up?* (7)

Activity development
● Hand out copies of photocopiable page 119. Read through the instructions with the group and identify whether they are fully understood (particularly the use of the word 'exactly').
● It may be worth ensuring all children use the same three colours, as this will make it easier for them to compare their flags.
● Pay particular attention to the first few completed flags, ensuring that the three stripes are filled in using solid blocks of colour (otherwise the task would be unnecessarily open).
● Identify whether or not the children apply systematic strategies. For example, they may select two colours initially and establish all possible combinations (6) before introducing a third colour.
● The photocopiable page does not contain enough flags to record all 18 combinations. The question at the foot of the sheet is designed to prompt individuals to draw further flags of their own. If you prefer, an additional copy of the sheet will allow continuation.
● Ask questions as the children progress through the task: *Is that flag different from that one? What will you do next? How many different flags do you think there will be? Have you found them all? How do you know?*

Review
● Establish that there are 18 different flags in total, with six possibilities for each combination of two colours. You could stress that looking at just two colours at a time breaks the task into smaller steps.
● Rather than simply going through the colour combinations for each flag, consider a numerical problem which is identical in structure. For example, provide a simple representation of a traffic light and explain that each must feature a combination of any two of the digits 1, 2 and 3. Begin by specialising with the digits 1 and 2, working through all six solutions (as shown left). Do the same for the digits 1 and 3 and for 2 and 3 (six solutions each; 18 in total). Work through the task as a group, directing questions at individual children as you follow through an orderly sequence.

Next steps
● Use the same photocopiable sheet but modify the conditions (for example, choose from only two colours and use one or both colours for each flag; this gives eight combinations).

Name

Flags

- Choose three colours for this challenge.
- Use exactly two colours to colour each flag. Each flag must be different.

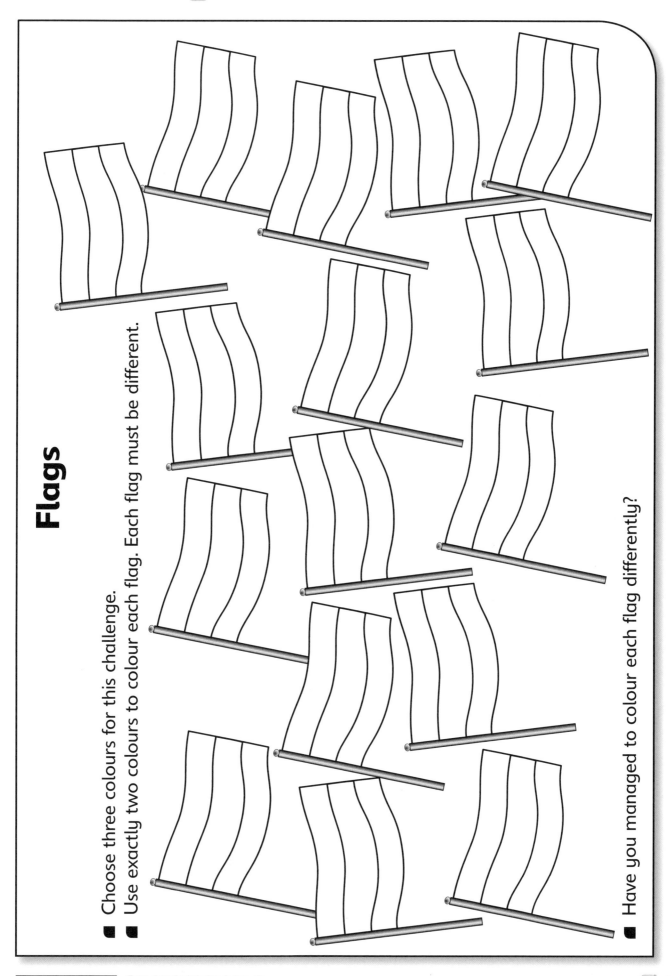

- Have you managed to colour each flag differently?

My day

Learning objectives
(Y4) Use/apply strand:
Report solutions to problems, giving explanations and reasoning orally and in writing.
(Y4) Data strand: Answer a question by identifying what data to collect; organise, present, analyse and interpret the data in tables, diagrams, tally charts, pictograms and bar charts, using ICT where appropriate.

Expected prior knowledge
● Tell the time.
● Estimate the approximate timing of key events/routines (for example, the time the school day begins and ends).

You will need
Wall calendar (optional); individual whiteboards; photocopiable page 121 (one per child); coloured pens/pencils.

Key vocabulary
morning, afternoon, day, night, 24 hours, month, seconds

Activity introduction
● Check the group's factual understanding of time, including the relationship between the different units of time.
● Ask questions: *How many seconds are there in one minute? How many hours are there in a day?*
● Revise the number of days in each month by referring to calendars or the rhyme '30 days hath September...'.

Activity development
● Begin with a discussion of routines on a school day. Focus the discussion on key events (such as bedtime), avoiding details of a relatively short duration (such as cleaning teeth).
● Provide individual whiteboards and ask questions relating to the children's timing of specific events. For example, say: *Write down the time you have lunch.*
● Give each child a copy of photocopiable page 121 and explain how the 12 at the top of this special clock relates to midnight. Continue by working round the 24 hours. Tell the children to begin the colouring of the sheet by shading round from the top to the point where they declare that they wake up. After that, advise them about the suitability of other key events in their day that could be labelled/coloured. Ask them to label each block of colour to explain what the event is.

Review
● Ask each child to 'show and tell' their ideas.
● Look to see how many hours the children spend sleeping. Talk about what fraction of a whole day this represents.

Next steps
● Consider repeating the activity for a day in the holidays. What differences are there?
● Take a strip of paper and use this to make a pictorial diary of the day. Consider adding a scale to register the passing of the 24 hours. By joining the ends to form a loop, the cyclical nature of a daily routine can be emphasised (see diagram below).

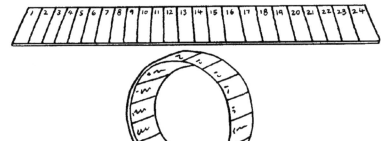

● Use a data-handling software package to present the length of different routines in different graphical formats (for example, bar charts).

My day

◾ How do you spend your day?

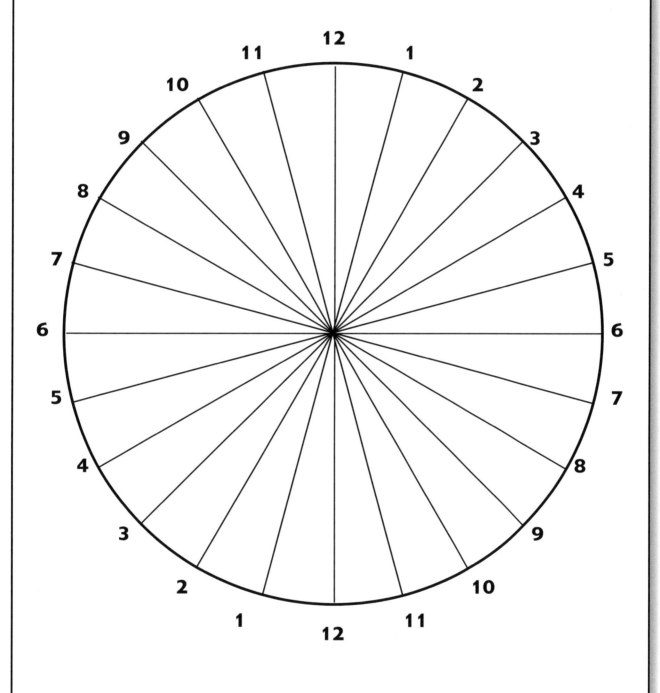

Out for six

Learning objectives
(Y3) Use/apply strand:
Follow a line of enquiry by deciding what information is important; make and use lists, tables and graphs to organise and interpret the information.
(Y5) Data strand: Describe the occurrence of familiar events, using the language of chance or likelihood.

Expected prior knowledge
● Add several single-digit numbers mentally, adding the sub-total to a running score (50 limit).

You will need
Coins (one per pair); photocopiable page 123 (one per pair); standard dice (one per pair); individual whiteboards.

Key vocabulary
probably, maybe, certain, impossible, even chance, fair

Brainteaser link
19: 'In the mix' on page 17.

Activity introduction
● Ask the children to 'invent' a chain of 20 coin tosses, listing heads and tails without the use of a coin. Now ask them to use a coin and list 20 actual tosses (as shown below).
Typical invented sequence:
T, H, T, T, H, H, T, H, T, T, H, T, H, T, H, T, H, H, T, T
An actual sequence:
T, H, H, H, T, T, H, T, T, T, T, T, H, H, T, H, T, T, H, T
● Working in pairs, ask the children to compare the lists. Ask them to consider the longest run of heads or tails in both lists. Typically, an inexperienced learner will underplay the potential for runs of three or more of the same outcome: use this knowledge to see if you can 'magically' distinguish between the children's invented and actual (empirical) lists.
● Try to introduce some of the language of probability (see 'Key vocabulary').

Activity development
● Provide each pair of children with a copy of photocopiable page 123. The game is for two players. Begin by heading the columns with the players' names and talk the children through the following rules.
● Player 1 rolls a standard dice and, unless they have thrown a 6, takes the number of points shown on the dice. Player 1 then decides whether to roll again or pass over to Player 2. A player can roll as many times as they want, unless they throw a 6.
● If a player throws a 6, their score for that round is zero.
● A player banks his/her score for each round and the winner is the player who achieves a running total which exceeds a (suggested) target figure of 50 points.
● The game requires players to have a growing understanding of risk (probability). They should also be able to maintain a score after each throw of the dice, and then add the total for each round to the overall points tally.
● Observe the children's ability to follow rules, to wait their turn, to calculate accurately and to keep satisfactorily on track of the recording.
● Ask questions: *What are you doing now? Are you going to risk another throw? What is the chance that this throw will be a 6?*

Review
● Create a vocabulary list of probability words used by yourself and the children.
● Discuss whether a high-risk strategy was more effective than a steadier accumulation of points. With the latter approach, what was a sensible number of throws in any one round?

Next steps
● Play with two dice, with the object being to avoid a difference of 0 (the probability of which is statistically the same as the probability of throwing a 6 was in the original game).

Name _____

Out for six

◧ Be the first to build a score of 50 points.

Player 1		Player 2	
Round total	Running total	Round total	Running total

◧ Remember: you don't want to roll a 6!

Double dice

Activity introduction

- Present an enlarged grid (see example right) to the children.

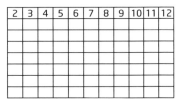

2	3	4	5	6	7	8	9	10	11	12

- Place a large counter alongside each numeral. Explain that each counter will move down one space if the number it represents is scored as the total of the two large dice. The two dice are repeatedly played until one of the counters reaches the end of the track.
- Play a couple of rounds to give the children time to appreciate the process, then abbreviate play with some focused questions: *Which counter do you predict will win? Is it a fair game? Are any of the numbers unlikely to win?*
- Continue play to the conclusion of the game. In all likelihood, a number towards the middle of the range will win (although this cannot be guaranteed). At this early stage of the lesson, you might simply want to suggest that, because there are more ways of making certain numbers, these have more chance of winning.

Activity development

- Provide each pair of children with photocopiable page 125, two dice and some counters or cubes (for covering totals as they are achieved).
- Point out that the two game boards feature different numbers and allocate one to each child. Note that the boards have been designed so that both players have a fair opportunity to win.
- Players take turns to roll the dice, with both individuals taking an active interest in the total. If one or both players have a number matching the total, it can be covered with a counter. Play continues until one player fills their board.
- You may find that, for some children, the competitive element overrides the mathematical considerations. In such cases, players can simply work together to see which board gets finished first.
- Encourage early finishers to play again. This will give further opportunity to gauge their appreciation of chance. Ask: *What numbers do you seem to get regularly? Why doesn't double 6 come up very often? Does it seem like a fair game?*

Review

- Discuss pairs' progress as a group, drawing out the mathematics as you go. Present a matrix (as shown left), completing this collectively to demonstrate why an outcome of 7 is the most likely.

Learning objectives
(Y3) Knowledge strand: Derive and recall all addition and subtraction facts for each number to 20.
(Y5) Data strand: Describe the occurrence of familiar events, using the language of chance or likelihood.

Expected prior knowledge
- All pairs with totals to 20.
- Collect and record data in lists and tables.

You will need
Enlarged grid (see activity introduction); 11 large counters; two large dice; photocopiable page 125 (one per pair); individual whiteboards; standard dice (two per pair); counters or cubes (at least nine per pair).

Key vocabulary
unlikely, total, fair, predict

Brainteaser link
19: 'In the mix' on page 17.

		First dice					
		1	**2**	**3**	**4**	**5**	**6**
	1	2	3	4	5	6	7
	2	3	4	5	6	7	8
Second dice	**3**	4	5	6	7	8	9
	4	5	6	7	8	9	10
	5	6	7	8	9	10	11
	6	7	8	9	10	11	12

Next steps
- Children can play the game again, this time copying blank game boards onto individual whiteboards and choosing their own numbers.
- Consider the difference between the numbers on a pair of dice (this ranges from 0 to 5; the largest difference, that between 6 and 1, is 5). Modify the matrix to consider which difference is the most likely (1 has ten combinations of dice outcomes, such as the difference between 3 and 2).

Double dice

- Roll two dice and find their total.
- See who is first to score all the totals on their game board.

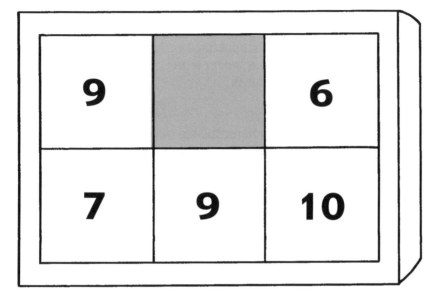

9		6
7	9	10

8	8	11
7		5

Dice mix

Learning objectives
(Y3) Knowledge strand:
Derive and recall
multiplication facts for the
2, 3, 4, 5, 6 and 10 times-
tables and the
corresponding division
facts.
(Y5) Data strand: Describe
the occurrence of familiar
events, using the language
of chance or likelihood.

**Expected prior
knowledge**
● Recall or quickly derive all
multiples of whole numbers
up to 6 × 6.

You will need
Photocopiable page 127
(one per pair); standard dice
(two per pair); counters or
cubes (at least nine per
pair); individual
whiteboards.

Key vocabulary
unlikely, total, fair, predict,
factors, multiples

Brainteaser link
19: 'In the mix' on page 17.

Activity introduction
● Ask some quick-fire questions about dice multiples, reinforcing the term 'product'. Discuss why it is that double 6 is so hard to achieve in a game situation, clarifying that there is only one combination out of many other unsuccessful combinations.
● Ask questions: *What is the product of 5 and 4? How might we get an answer of 6? Can you think of another way?*
● If time permits, you could start listing some of the possible product outcomes as a list of number pairs (beginning with '1, 1') or as a matrix (see right).

		First dice					
		1	**2**	**3**	**4**	**5**	**6**
	1	1	2	3	4	5	6
	2	2	4	6	8	10	12
Second	**3**	3	6	9	12	15	18
dice	**4**	4	8	12	16	20	24
	5	5	10	15	20	25	30
	6	6	12	18	24	30	36

Activity development
● Provide each pair with photocopiable page 127, two dice and a handful of counters or cubes (for covering answers as they are achieved).
● Point out that the two game boards feature different numbers, and allocate one to each child. Note that the boards have been designed so that both players have a fair opportunity to win.
● Players take turns to roll the dice, with both individuals taking an active interest in the total. If one or both players have a number matching the product, it can be covered with a counter. Play continues until one player fills their board.
● Observe the different calculation strategies used by each child. In particular, look for children who still routinely calculate answers by counting on from zero.
● Encourage early finishers to play again. This will give further opportunity to gauge the children's appreciation of chance. Ask: *What numbers do you seem to get regularly? Why doesn't double 1 come up very often? Does it seem like a fair game?*

Review
● Discuss pairs' progress as a group, drawing out the mathematics as you go. Complete the matrix as shown above, identifying those numbers which feature most frequently (for example, 12).
● Use the language of multiples and factors, confirming that it is those numbers with the most factors (within the constraints of the dice) which are most likely to be generated.
● Note that an outcome of 16, while having multiple factors in an open situation, has only a 1 in 36 chance of being generated within the confines of this game.

Next steps
● Children can play the game again, this time copying blank game boards onto individual whiteboards and choosing their own numbers.
● The matrix can be used to begin to quantify the likelihood of a particular event happening. The probability of scoring 20, for example, is 2 in 36 (or 1 in 18).

Dice mix

◼ Throw the dice and calculate the product of the two dice.

◼ See who is first to score all the products on their game board.

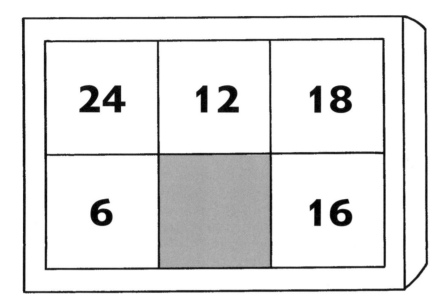

24	12	18
6		16

20	15	9
30		12